DATE DUE

Dec 13 '72			
Dec 11 '73			
GAYLORD M-2			PRINTED IN U.S.A.

Galdós and the Creative Process

BENITO PÉREZ GALDÓS

and the Creative Process

by WALTER T. PATTISON

University of Minnesota Press, Minneapolis

PRINTED AT THE LUND PRESS, INC., MINNEAPOLIS

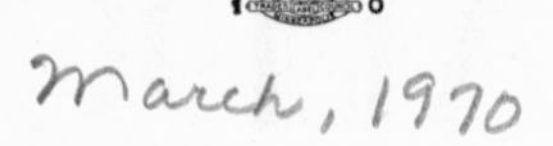

Library of Congress Catalog Card Number: 54-10291

PUBLISHED IN GREAT BRITAIN, INDIA, AND PAKISTAN BY
GEOFFREY CUMBERLEGE: OXFORD UNIVERSITY PRESS, LONDON, BOMBAY, AND KARACHI

TO

A. M. P.

WITH FILIAL GRATITUDE AND AFFECTION

ACKNOWLEDGMENTS

ON GIVING this book to the press I recall with pleasure the numerous friends both in the United States and Spain who have generously contributed to the information which will be found within its covers.

To list all of their names here would be a gratifying, but at the same time a long and perhaps superfluous task – many of their names appear in the text and footnotes. To all of them I extend again my deep appreciation.

I must make an exception of some whose names do not appear elsewhere. Marion Zeitlin and John Crow read a part of the manuscript and encouraged me in the pursuit of this subject. Hermann Ramras offered many helpful suggestions for clarifying the wording of my final text. I can only hope that my study justifies the confidence they felt in it and the efforts they made on my behalf.

W. T. P.

University of Minnesota
August 1954

CONTENTS

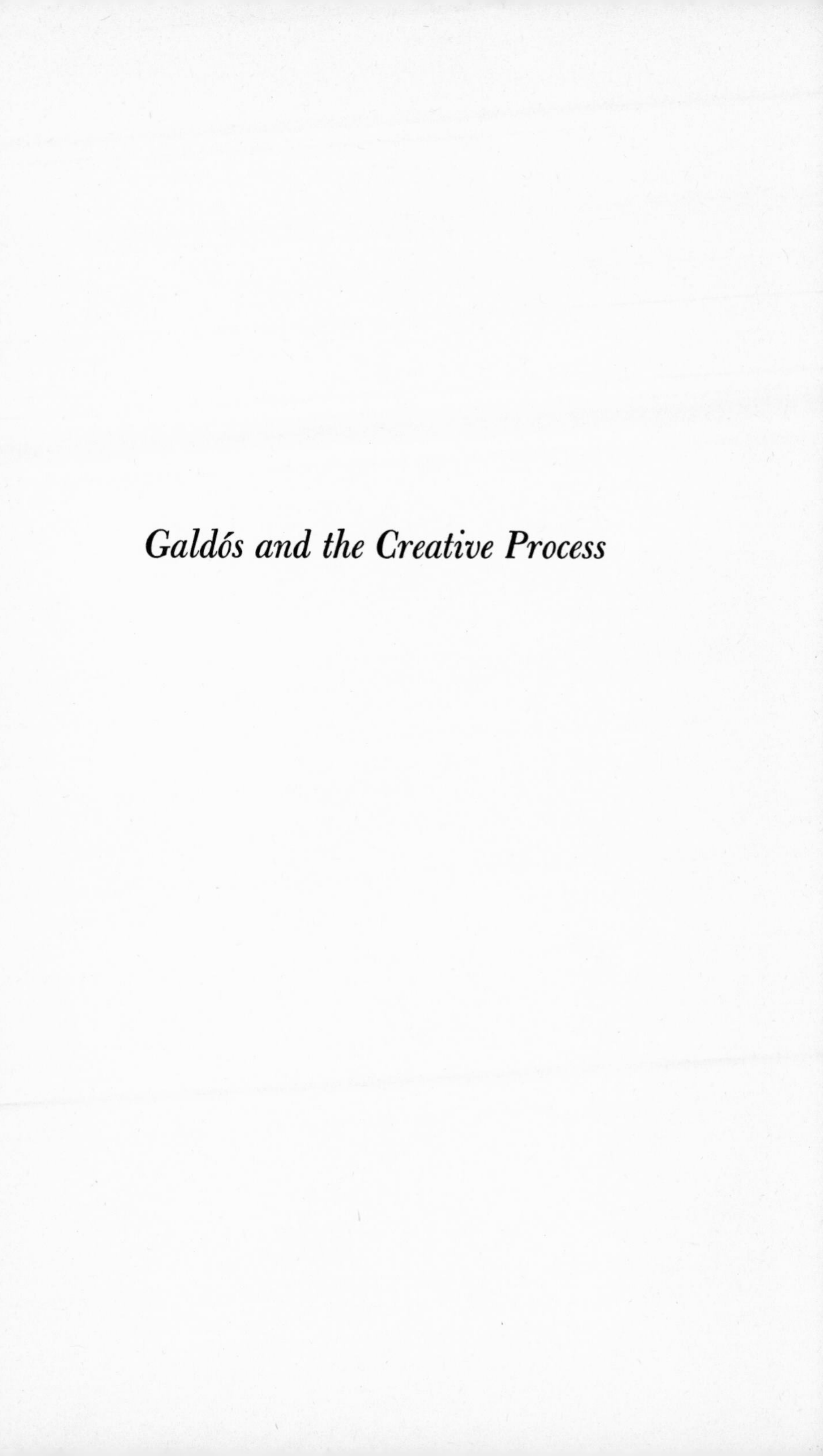

Galdós and the Creative Process

INTRODUCTION

Benito Pérez Galdós is a great novelist — so great, in fact, that most critics would place him second only to Cervantes in the world of Spanish letters. As a figure of such stature he of course merits investigations into all aspects of his life and work; but strangely enough, relatively few scholars have chosen him as their theme. His Spanish compatriots have allowed his letters to go unpublished; most of his journalism remains uncollected; his novels await adequate analysis. What work has been done is largely the tribute of foreign admirers.

My interest in this remarkable novelist has been long-standing, but only in the last few years have I attempted to apply to his productions some of the techniques of literary analysis successfully developed by the critics of French and English literature. It is obviously presumptuous to pretend to explain, or perhaps even to discuss, the creative process of a genius. I do not believe a complete explanation can ever be reached. Yet I think it possible to narrow down the area of the unknown, and this is essentially the task I am setting myself with respect to two Galdosian novels — *Gloria* and *Marianela.* Many elements of these novels do not depend upon creative imagination but can be traced back to real-life people or places or again to literary sources; many ideas which we might at first believe original with Galdós find frequent expression in the magazines he read. So by a detailed study of what Galdós was reading and observing before composing these particular novels, I hope to reduce in size, but not eliminate, the central core of mystery which must always defy the efforts of the scholar.

In a sense the discovery of the specific origin of various factors in the novels continues the old-fashioned "source studies," but this is by no means all I hope to do. There are numerous elements for which no definite source can be named, yet which can be related to the thought of the times. But above all I hope to show some reasons why and how this material was assembled into artistic form – why, for example, the author was impelled to write on religion in *Gloria*, how and why he looked for certain types of material, and how the associative bonds between these materials led him to recombine them in a new, original form. As the answers to these questions take us into speculative areas our results are of course more uncertain; but as these same questions are the fundamental problems of the creative process, we shall penetrate it to the extent that we find the answers.

One great advantage which I have had over previous students of Galdós was the opportunity to examine thoroughly all the markings and notes in the books of Galdós' personal library. In the winter of 1950–1951, the great author's daughter, Doña María Galdós de Verde, kindly gave me access to her home in Madrid where all these books are now housed. The monotonous task of copying all the markings sometimes seemed to be a waste of time, as often while doing this routine work I had no idea what relationship existed between the pencilings and Galdós' original works. Yet later it became apparent that many marked passages had been sought out precisely as preparation for some one of the novels.

Literary creation is held to be something superior to mere handicraft; the very word "creation" links it metaphorically with both the life process and the world beginnings, just as the author is seen as the "father" of his fictitious characters or as the god-like genius which drew them out of nothingness. Yet here I believe that metaphors lead to hazy thinking. Literary creation – we cannot avoid the word – brings forth nothing tangible but operates in the sphere of the imagination. It is a mental process, and we must seek its laws in the realm of psychology. We may assume that the creative mind follows the same psychological patterns as other minds. I hope that some information on the operation of the mind of one specific author will be forthcoming in the following pages. In the final analysis, our failure to reach an absolute answer to the problem of artistic creation is linked to our inability to comprehend fully the human thought processes.

FORMATIVE PERIOD: FOREIGN INFLUENCES

At the age of nineteen Benito Pérez Galdós left his home in the Canary Islands to study law in Madrid. From his nineteenth to his thirtieth year – that is, from 1862 to 1873 – he was, perhaps without realizing it, preparing for his career as a novelist. He lived in the capital, soon dropping his formal university studies and becoming a fledgling journalist. Finally he turned to fiction, and after three youthful trials, he began to novelize the history of nineteenth-century Spain in his *Episodios Nacionales*. The first twenty of these historical novels were produced between 1873 and 1879. But at the same time that Galdós devoted himself to history, he gave thought to the contemporary scene, which he depicted in *Doña Perfecta*, *Gloria*, *Marianela*, and *La familia de León Roch*. Two of these novels of contemporary affairs are the subject of my investigations in the following chapters, in which I try to shed more light on the currents of thought which the author combined in their production, or, in other words, on some aspects of Galdós' creative process.

Before dealing with these two specific novels, I want to examine in broader terms literary influences which were coming to bear upon the young novelist. This is possible on the basis of his autobiographical writings, such as his *Memorias*, of the hidden autobiographical references in his novels – especially in the later volumes of the *Episodios Nacionales*, which picture the years when Galdós was serving his literary apprenticeship in Madrid – and finally on the basis of an examination of Galdós' private library, where the literary preferences and enthusiasms of the writer are often revealed by the number of volumes of a given author and the amount of penciling and annotations they provoked.

We know by Galdós' direct testimony that he delighted to read works of other novelists,[1] and that among his early idols were Balzac[2] and Dickens.[3] His first acquaintance with Balzac was through *Eugénie Grandet*, which he bought in a bookstall by the Seine in the summer of 1867. During his visits to Paris in the summer of that year and the next, he acquired and read the entire *Comédie Humaine*. Galdós also informs us that his devotion to Dickens began shortly after his acquaintance with Balzac.

These statements can be substantiated by looking at the Spanish author's library.[4] He in fact possessed the *Comedie Humaine* and a large collection of Dickens in both English and French.[5] As for the dates of his first readings – and Galdós was notoriously inaccurate in dating his personal history – they too are upheld by other evidence. Galdós names a Balzacian character, Klaes, in his earliest novel (*La Sombra*), written about 1866–1867 but not published until 1870. In *La Nación* of March 9, 1868, he published a very laudatory essay on Dickens showing first-hand knowledge of his work. In the essay are several incidental allusions to Balzac, all praising him. Twice Dickens' technique is compared to Balzac's (and there are no comparisons to any

[1] *Obras completas*, Aguilar, VI, 1509.

[2] *Ibid.*, p. 1730.

[3] *Ibid.*, p. 1768.

[4] As mentioned in the first chapter, through the kindness of Doña María Galdós de Verde I had the opportunity to examine all the books in Galdós' private library. I wish to thank her here for her friendly cooperation. Recently a catalogue of the library has been published, a posthumous work of the late H. Chonon Berkowitz (*La biblioteca de Benito Pérez Galdós*, El Museo Canario, 1951). Through the kindness of William H. Shoemaker I had the opportunity of examining this catalogue in manuscript before my trip to Madrid (1950–1951) where I studied the markings in the volumes.

[5] Berkowitz, *La biblioteca de Benito Pérez Galdós*, pp. 178 and 188–189.

other authors), showing that Galdós held Balzac almost as a measure of excellence at this time. In the same number of *La Nación* Galdós' translation of Pickwick Papers begins.[6]

The facts I have presented so far are generally known and accepted. But a far more interesting and detailed knowledge of Galdós' literary passions can be had by the proper interpretation of a certain autobiographical passage in the last series of *Episodios Nacionales.* Fortunately, a comparison of the readings of a Galdosian character with the books in Galdós' personal library enables us to ascertain the extent to which the character's readings are the same as those of the author himself.

Before looking at this passage, it is well to note the many other autobiographical elements in the same series of historical novels. They indicate that Galdós was drawing heavily on his own youthful experiences in preparing these works. A few examples: Ibero's experiences in Paris during the World's Fair of 1867 parallel those of Galdós;[7] a number of sessions of the Cortes Constituyentes[8] are viewed by fictitious characters from the balcony where Galdós himself witnessed them; the protagonist of *Amadeo I* is a journalist who worked for papers like *El Debate* for which Galdós himself wrote and who made his first trip to Santander in the summer of 1871 just as Galdós did; one of his characters is interested in raising chickens[9] as was the author himself; the Café Universal, where the Canary Islanders, with Galdós among them, gathered for their *tertulia,*

[6] Although the translation is anonymous, Galdós acknowledges it as his own in his *Memorias* (*Obras completas,* VI, 1768). But the statement in *La Nación* that the translation was made from the English original is incorrect. In Galdós' library is a copy of *Aventures de Monsieur Pickwick* (par Ch. Dickens. Roman anglais traduit avec l'autorisation de l'auteur sous la direction de P. Lorain par P. Grolier. Tome premier. Paris, Hachette, 1865). On the half-title page we find written: "Se autoriza la traducción de esta novela. El censor," below which the official stamp of the Fiscalia de Novelas appears. A comparison of Galdós' translation with this French text and the English original shows that the Spanish follows the French rather than the English.

[7] *La de los tristes destinos,* Chap. 21.

[8] *España sin rey,* Chaps. 8, 10, and 12; *España trágica,* Chap. 1.

[9] *España trágica,* Chap. 8.

was haunted by Vicente Halconero and his friends.[10] Many other examples could be cited. We conclude that there is a strong possibility that any fictitious element in these novels may be a recollection of Galdós' own life.

Now Vicente Halconero, the hero of *España trágica* who is modeled in one detail at least on Galdós himself, is a voracious reader. Especially following the Revolution of 1868, when censorship no longer hindered the free importation of foreign literature, Vicente spent all his available funds in the Librería de Durán, later the Librería Fernando Fe, a house specializing in the importation of foreign books, which offered a fascinating novelty to the Spaniards and intoxicated them with the heady wine of new European ideas.[11] Galdós gives a rather detailed list of Vicente's reading, which I shall have to quote at length:

> Las primeras borracheras las tomó el neófito con Victor Hugo, que en verso y prosa le entusiasmaba y enloquecía. Vino luego Lamartine con sus dramáticos *Girondinos*; siguieron Thiers con *El Consulado y el Imperio*, y Michelet con sus admirables *Historias*. En su fiebre de asimilación empalmaba la Filosofía con la Literatura, y tan pronto se asomaba con ardiente anhelo a la selva encantada de Balzac, *La comedia humana*, como se metía en el inmenso laberinto de Laurent, *Historia de la Humanidad*. Por complacer a su padrastro, don Angel Cordero, apechugó con Bastiat y otros pontífices de la Economía política, y para quitar el amargor de estas áridas lecturas, se entretuvo con la socarronería burguesa del *Jerónimo Paturot*.
>
> Impelido por intensa curiosidad, dedicóse el incipiente lector a los maestros alemanes. Devoró a Goethe y Schiller; se enredó luego con Enrique Heine, *Atta Troll*, *Reisebilder*, y por esta curva germánica volvió a Francia con Teófilo Gautier, Janin, Vacquerie, que le llevaron de nuevo a la espléndida flora de Victor Hugo. Mayores estímulos de sed ardiente le empujaron hacia Rousseau y Voltaire, de donde saltó de un brinco a las constelaciones de la antigüedad clásica. Homero, Virgilio, Esquilo, el cual, como por la mano, le condujo hacia el espléndido grupo estelario de Shakespeare: *Otelo*, *Hamlet*, *Romeo y Julieta*. De aquí, por derivaciones puramente caprichosas, fué a parar a *Jorge*

[10] *Ibid.*, Chap. 10.
[11] *Ibid.*, Chap. 1.

Sand, Enrique Murger, y al desvergonzado Paul de Kock. El espíritu del neófito se remontó de improviso, requiriendo arte y emociones de mayor vuelo. Releyó historias y poemas, y buscando, al fin, con la belleza, la amargura que a su alma era grata, se refugió en *Werther*, como en una silenciosa gruta llena de maravillas geológicas, y ornada con arborizantes parietarias de peregrina hermosura.

No tardó Halconero en tomar grande afición a la literatura concebida y expuesta en forma personal: las llamadas Memorias, relato más o menos artificioso de acaecimientos verídicos, o las invenciones que para suplantar a la realidad se revisten del disfraz autobiográfico, ya diluyendo en cartas toda una historia sentimental, ya consignando en diarios apuntes las sucesivas borrascas de un corazón atormentado. En densas epístolas puso Rousseau su *Nueva Eloísa*, y en espasmos de amor y desesperación, diariamente trasladados al papel, contó Goethe las desdichas del enamorado de Carlota.[12]

To what extent is this passage a reflection of Galdós' own reading? The testimony of his private library shows, I believe, that Vicente Halconero's youthful reading was identical to that of Benito Pérez Galdós. Many of the authors cited above are represented in the Spanish novelist's personal library. Often their works are marked in a manner indicating the interest of their possessor. The marking is particularly significant because Galdós as a rule did not mark books of belles-lettres.[13] Many small indications point to the conclusion that such markings as we find in them were done in his early formative period.[14] Let us see specifically how the authors of the above citation are represented in Galdós' library.

Of Victor Hugo's poetry he had *Odes et ballades* (Paris, 1862), which edition includes the *Feuilles d'Automne* and the *Chants du crépuscule*, *Les orientales* (Paris, 1862), and a volume con-

[12] *Ibid.*

[13] Berkowitz, *op. cit.*, p. 13.

[14] Some books were bound after notes and marginal translations had been made, as is evident from the fact that the ends of some of the notes were trimmed off in the process; others have stickers with Galdós' name and a place for a catalogue number. None of the works in these two categories was printed after 1876, about which time I think the novelist tried to put his library in order.

taining *Les voix intérieures* and *Les rayons et les ombres* (Paris, 1859).[15] In these tomes many passages are marked. At the present time the Galdós library contains but three prose works of Hugo. Of these the most interesting is *Nuestra señora de París* (in a collection of three novels beginning with Fernández y González' *Don Alvaro de Luna*). Here Galdós has inscribed on page 109 an ornate "B" similar to the initials which we find in his school textbooks.[16] The other prose works of Hugo are *Bug-Jargal* in two editions and *Napoleon le petit.*[17] The latter is not marked. I shall try to show later that Galdós must have known the immensely popular *Les misérables*, which enjoyed great fame in Madrid at the time when the young author reached that city.[18] For the moment, let us recall that Galdós, in an article written in 1868, calls Hugo one of the five great *novelists* (not *poets*) of the nineteenth century.[19]

Although the Galdós library at present contains eleven works of Lamartine,[20] the only one in which I noted any marks was precisely the one named in Vicente Halconero's reading list, *Historia de los Girondinos* (Madrid, 1851–1852). The singling out of this work in both the library and the list is significant.

The next two authors, Thiers and Michelet, are not represented in Galdós' library. As Berkowitz has well observed, many books must have disappeared from it, for Galdós was notably easygoing and generous with his personal property.[21] But these specific works of Michelet and Thiers were probably never in his personal library for the simple reason that they were enormous and consequently costly. Thiers' *Histoire du Consulat et*

[15] Berkowitz, *op. cit.*, p. 178.

[16] *Ibid.*, p. 137.

[17] *Ibid.*, pp. 181 and 72.

[18] Berkowitz, *Pérez Galdós – Spanish Liberal Crusader*, p. 55.

[19] "Carlos Dickens," *La Nación*, March 9, 1868.

[20] Berkowitz, *La biblioteca de Benito Pérez Galdós*, pp. 72–73 and 181.

[21] *Ibid.*, p. 12. We can prove that many books were lost by examining those which bear Galdós' early catalogue numbers. Although these serial numbers run at least as high as 204 (see below, note 35), only about a dozen of the works so catalogued are still in the library. One specific case of a lost book is Marliani, *Combate de Trafalgar* (Madrid, 1850), which Galdós acquired as material for *Trafalgar* (see *Memorias*, *Obras completas*, VI, 1734), but which is no longer in the collection.

de l'Empire filled twenty volumes; Michelet's *Histoire de France* comprised seventeen volumes and his *Histoire de la révolution française* seven more! Galdós did have some of the shorter works of these men,[22] but their long histories he probably read in the library of the Ateneo.

The reading list in *España trágica* next mentions Balzac, on whom we need say no more. But the account goes on to state that Vicente read philosophy along with literature, a thing which I intend to show was true of Don Benito[23] but which has been doubted by as competent a critic as Berkowitz, precisely because the Spaniard's library contained so few philosophical works.[24] In *España trágica* we have cited Laurent's *Etudes sur l'histoire de l'humanité* (Bruxelles, 1861–1870, eighteen volumes). The work in question is not well described by its title; it is actually a history of ideas, stressing the philosophical and religious concepts especially of nineteenth-century thinkers. Galdós is right in calling it an "inmenso laberinto." From it and from the Ateneo lectures and discussions he could, and probably did, get a good working knowledge of modern philosophy. At the present time, only the first volume of Laurent's compendium is preserved in the novelist's library and it shows no markings.[25] It is a pity that the later tomes have disappeared, as they may have had more direct influence on some of Galdós' creations.[26]

In *España trágica*, a few pages after the reading list we have been checking, Galdós gives us a short supplement. His young hero keeps on buying foreign books from Durán's shop, "y anhelando nutrir su pensamiento con doctrinas fundamentales, recibió de manos del mercader importador las obras de Ahrems [*sic*; read *Ahrens*] y de Spencer. Cargó luego con lo último de Proudhon y con *La Democracia en América* de Tocqueville, libro que volvía locos a todos los políticos de aquel tiempo."[27] This

[22] Berkowitz, *La biblioteca de Benito Pérez Galdós,* pp. 39, 46, and 68.
[23] See pp. 37–39 and 47–52.
[24] Berkowitz, *La biblioteca de Benito Pérez Galdós,* p. 14.
[25] *Ibid.*, p. 73.
[26] See p. 52, n. 116.
[27] *España trágica,* Chap. 6.

is important to us now because it enlarges the list of books under the heading of "philosophy" that we have just been examining.

Strictly speaking, only the first of the four men is what we would call a philosopher today, the others being more naturally classed as sociologists, but in the nineteenth century all were considered in the former category. Ahrens was a Belgian interpreter of Krause, whose importance for Galdós and Spain we shall investigate later. None of his works was in Galdós' library. Spencer and Proudhon were well represented.[28] However, of the works of these two men only one is marked, i.e., Herbert Spencer's *De la educación intelectual, moral y física* (translated by Siro García del Mazo, n.d.). De Tocqueville's thoughtful examination of the United States is not among the books in the present-day Galdós collection.

This brief review of Halconero's readings in philosophy leads us to the conclusion that both he and Galdós knew the contemporary trends and read the outstanding works, but that their interest in philosophy was that of an intelligent and curious amateur rather than an erudite professional.

Next we see that Vicente Halconero turned rather unwillingly to economics and read various authorities, of whom only Bastiat is named. This writer is not represented in Galdós' library but is mentioned by our author in a youthful essay[29] (as well as in later novels) in terms which indicate some knowledge of the nature of his work. This heavy reading was counterbalanced with the humor of Louis Reybaud's *Jérôme Paturot à la recherche d'une position sociale*, a book which is not today in Galdós' library.

The hero of *España trágica* now dips into German literature and devours Goethe, Schiller, and Heine. The works of these authors were possessed and copiously marked by Galdós.[30] They

[28] Berkowitz, *La biblioteca de Benito Pérez Galdós*, pp. 39, 49, 53, 58, and 64.

[29] "José Echegaray" in *Las Cortes*, May 12, 1869, and in *El Correo de España*, Sept. 27, 1870. In neither case is the article signed by Galdós, but I hope to show that it was his in another study.

[30] These three men are the only German authors represented by more than two books apiece in the Galdós library. See Berkowitz, *La biblioteca*

are particularly significant for us in our later studies, as Heine, especially through his *Reisebilder* mentioned here specifically, had something to do with the creation of *Gloria* and Goethe contributed to the formation of *Marianela*.

Then Vicente Halconero's interest shifts from German back to French literature. He reads Gautier, Janin, and Vacquerie,[31] rereads Hugo, and takes up Rousseau and Voltaire.[32]

There followed an immersion in Greek and Roman literature, among whose authors Homer, Virgil, and Aeschylus are specifically named. Galdós became interested in ancient literature as a student at the Universidad Central, principally through his admiration for three professors – Camús, Bardón, and Fernando de Castro – who gave courses in Latin literature, Greek, and ancient history. We have laudatory descriptions of all of these men from Galdós' pen.[33] His library was well stocked with Greek and Latin productions – mostly in translations.[34] Galdós marked passages and noted briefly the contents of some cantos of his *Homère* (Paris, 1863). He penciled only *Les Perses* in his *Théâtre d'Eschyle* (Paris, 1865).

I have not found markings in his copies of Virgil, but he did call attention to passages in Plutarch (French translation by

de Benito Pérez Galdós, pp. 173–174. Among Goethe's works, the following are marked: *Wilhelm Meister*, *Le Renard*, and *Théâtre*. There are many marked passages in Schiller's *Théâtre*. Heine's *Poëmes et Légendes* (Paris, 1869), which volume includes *Atta Troll* and *L'Intermezzo*, is penciled in many places; the same is true of *Reisebilder – Tableaux de voyage* (Paris, 1863). As Galdós mentions Heine in youthful articles (see page 98, n. 328) it is evident that he came to know the German poet earlier than his fictitious hero of *España trágica*. Another Galdosian character, Maxi Rubín, also read Goethe and Heine in about the same epoch (*c.* 1870) that Vicente Halconero discovered them (see *Obras completas*, Aguilar, V, 179).

[31] In Galdós' library we find Gautier, *Romans et contes*, Paris, 1874 (marked); Janin, *Un coeur pour deux amours*, Paris, 1869 (not marked) – Galdós must also have known this author by his witty chronicles in the *Revue des deux mondes*; and Vacquerie, *Profils et grimaces*, Paris, 1856 (not marked).

[32] Rousseau's complete works (not marked) appear in Galdós' library, but we find nothing by Voltaire. But even as early as 1883 Galdós had a mask of Voltaire in his study. (See article on Galdós by "El Doctor Fausto," i.e., Tolosa Latour, in *La Época*, Mar. 26, 1883.)

[33] Articles in *La Nación*, Feb. 8, 1866; Jan. 26, 1868; and Feb. 16, 1868.

[34] See Berkowitz, *La biblioteca de Benito Pérez Galdós*, pp. 186, 194–196.

A. Pierron, Paris, 1858); Ovid's *Les fastes* . . . (traduction par Mm. Th. Burette et Vernadé, Paris, n.d.); and Cicero's *Obras completas* (translated by M. Menéndez y Pelayo, Madrid, 1879). We should, to complete our estimate of his interest in classical antiquity, notice that he marked one passage in A. Pierron's *Histoire de la littérature romaine* (Paris, 1857), a few passages in V. Duruy's *Histoire grecque* (Paris, 1876),[35] and many places (mostly in the section on the Iberian peninsula) in Manuel M. A. y Rives' *Geografía histórica de la edad antigua* (Madrid, 1874).

We conclude that Galdós had a genuine interest in ancient literature, although he regularly read it in translation. His interest in it did not die with the end of his university studies, for a number of classical authors appear in editions from the 1870s. After this decade it is doubtful that Galdós bought much classical literature; and the new accessions to his library in that field are, in the main, gifts to the now famous novelist. We can say that the interests of Vicente Halconero and of Benito Pérez Galdós parallel one another in respect to classical literature.

The next place in Vicente's reading list is occupied by Shakespeare. Here again Galdós' library shows his enthusiasm for the author cited in the novel. Of the numerous editions of the bard of Avon,[36] the many markings in Emile Montégut's French translation (1867–1869) show that this was the form in which Galdós habitually read the English dramatist. The English texts (Bell's Edition, 1774) bear pencil lines in the two plays *Romeo and Juliet* and *Hamlet*, and the latter contains a number of marginal translations, showing that our novelist had been through it. None of the other editions is marked by Galdós, although the Guizot translation has marginal translations in another hand.

From English, Halconero comes back again to French literature, now discovering George Sand, Murger, and Paul de Kock. The first of these writers is represented in the Galdós library

[35] In Pierron's work Galdós' bookplate carries the serial number "N° 46"; Duruy's is "N° 204." The scheme of classification was not extended to the whole library. It was apparently done not long after 1876 (the date of Duruy's book) and then abandoned.

[36] Berkowitz, *La biblioteca de Benito Pérez Galdós*, pp. 191–192.

by three separate novels and her *Oeuvres complètes*, and of the latter, volume one, *Histoire de ma vie*, has been cut. Murger's famous *Scènes de la vie de Bohême* (1864) is there and was heavily marked and annotated by Galdós. Paul de Kock does not appear, but the extreme popularity of this author in Spain suggests that Galdós read him and that if he once possessed his works they may have disappeared in the hands of unscrupulous borrowers.[37]

At this point in the reading list Galdós remembers that Halconero has been, and is going to be, depicted repeatedly throughout *España trágica* as a young romantic. Consequently he stresses his interest in *Werther*, and in this I believe he begins to abandon the autobiographical parallels between himself and his creation. Yet he does bring in one more similarity. Halconero begins to read autobiographies and memoirs, both real and fictitious. No titles are cited, but we seem to have a reflection of the numerous works of personal history, usually heavily marked, in Galdós' library. These were obviously read as preparation for the *Episodios Nacionales*, although perhaps chronologically the interest in them developed before the concept of a series of historical novels. In any case, Galdós must have started reading them before 1873 when he began the series. On this point, too, there is a reflection of his own reading in that of his fictitious hero.

Of course not everything that the novelist read is repeated in the list attributed to his hero. Yet there is in it enough to allow us to lay down certain general conclusions. First, Galdós' interest in foreign literature, although extant before 1868, received a great stimulus from the revocation of censorship laws by the revolution in September of that year. He frequented Durán's bookshop, the chief purveyor of foreign literature in Madrid.[38] He bought and read many French authors and a few

[37] On the popularity of de Kock, see Joaquín M. Sanromá's *Mis memorias* (Madrid, 1887).

[38] Juanito Santa Cruz, another Galdosian hero, bought great quantities of books from the establishment of Bailly-Baillière, which also imported foreign literature. His interest in reading came at about the same date as Vicente Halconero's (see *Obras completas*, Aguilar, V, 14). In another

English[39] and German ones, and he continued his readings in classical literatures. About this time he also developed a great interest in personal histories.

All in all, Galdós must have been a very busy young man in the period from about 1867 to 1873. The amount of reading he did was in itself no small task. Besides this he was very active in journalism, even being editor of a daily paper, *El Debate*, in 1871 and of one of the chief literary reviews of Spain in 1872. Furthermore, he produced his first novels, *La fontana de oro*, *El audaz*, and *La sombra*, in this period, to say nothing of his early dramas. I cannot agree with Berkowitz in his statement that Galdós was then living in a trance.[40] Rather I would compare this period to a renaissance, a fertilization of one literature by contacts with others, although in this case it is a personal, one-man renaissance.

How his contact with foreign literature brought about new creations in the Spanish novel is the subject of the next two chapters.

novel – *El Doctor Centeno* – the university students read Balzac, Hugo, and Schiller (*ibid.*, pp. 1366, 1367, 1368, and 1374). The action of this novel is supposed to occur in 1863–1864 (*ibid.*, pp. 1289 and 1419) and it seems to reflect many of Galdós' own experiences.

[39] The only English writers possessed in any quantity by Galdós were Shakespeare, Dickens, Scott, and Goldsmith. No other author is represented by more than two works.

[40] Berkowitz, *Pérez Galdós – Spanish Liberal Crusader*, p. 90. The statement is based on Galdós' *Memorias* (*Obras completas*, Aguilar, VI, 1734): "Dejadme ahora en mi sueño cataléptico . . . Siento pasar el 70, el 71, y a mediados del 72 vuelvo a la vida . . ." But earlier in the same work (*ibid.*, p. 1729), when Galdós feared that many events of his life would escape his memory and that perhaps he should desist from writing his memoirs, he says to himself: "Simplón, no temas dar a la publicidad los recuerdos que salgan luminosos de tu fatigado cerebro, y abandona los que se obstinen en quedar agazapados en el seno del olvido, que ello será como si una parte de mi existencia sufriese temporal muerte o catalepsia . . ." Galdós was not in a trance; he simply could not remember at the time anything worth relating from the years 1870–1872.

THE GENESIS OF *GLORIA*

INTRODUCTION

ACCORDING to Galdós' own words, his novel *Gloria* was the result of a sudden flash of inspiration. One day in December 1876, as he walked in the Puerta del Sol on the short stretch of sidewalk between the Calle de la Montera and the Café Universal, the complete plan of the first volume of the novel flashed into his mind. The second volume, in a sense a sequel not necessary to the understanding of the theme, was not the result of inspiration, but was patiently contrived. Galdós wished later that he had not written it. The only reason that he produced it at all was that a certain critic urged him to wring the theme dry and to underline the moral of the story.[1]

Galdós was in general impatient with people who tried to pry into his creative process. He usually replied that the idea of a work "just came to him," which was the quickest way of stopping further questions.[2] His statement on the origin of *Gloria* is a little more explicit, since after all it had been requested by his good friend and critical champion, Clarín, but essentially it turns aside curiosity with the same device. The idea of *Gloria* "just came to him" by inspiration.

But if we think that inspiration provided the theme of religious

[1] This is told by Clarín on the basis of a letter from Galdós. See Leopoldo Alas (Clarín), *Galdós* (*Obras completas,* Tomo primero), Madrid, 1912, p. 28.

[2] H. Chonon Berkowitz, *Pérez Galdós – Spanish Liberal Crusader*, p. 104.

conflict, the plot, characters, and setting, without any relation to what Galdós had been seeing and hearing about him, I think that we should be far from any comprehension of the nature of inspiration or the creative process. The creative imagination works on and with the store of material already in the artist's mind, "for a work of pure imagination is not something fabricated by a *tour de force* from nothing, and suspended, without anchorage in fact, in the impalpable ether of a visionary world." [3]

As Lowes goes on to show in the work just cited, a poet assembles, by subconscious associations, a small part of the mass of impressions he has stored away; he culls and rejects those which do not blend with the emotional tone of his projected work, he may even add to his wealth by seeking direct experience or indirectly by reading, and finally he amalgamates and fuses these materials into a work of art. If he is a master artist the parts are so welded that the seams can scarcely be detected; if he is less skilled the joints are visible and the matter is juxtaposed rather than fused together.

The inspiration which Galdós felt as he approached his favorite *café* was the moment of crystallization when a whole series of stored-up impressions fell into a pattern. The right elements fitted into the right places; nothing then remained but to set the result down on paper, which Galdós did in an enthusiastic two weeks.[4]

Goethe has described similar experiences for us. He tells that when he received the news of a friend's suicide, "at that instant the plan of *Werther* was found; the whole shot together from all directions, and became a solid mass, as the water in a vase,

[3] John L. Lowes, *The Road to Xanadu*, Boston, Houghton Mifflin, 1927, p. 241. The same thought was expressed in 1879 by M. de la Revilla, who, talking about works of pure imagination, says: "Cierto que estas creaciones, cuando al mundo real se refieren, tienen su base en la realidad y son combinaciones de datos de la experiencia, elaborados y compuestos en maravillosa síntesis por las facultades creadoras del artista; pero si están compuestos con elementos de la realidad, la composición de estos elementos, la síntesis de estos elementos y factores son creación libre del artista." See *Revista de España*, 68 (1879), 174.

[4] "*Gloria* fué obra de un entusiasmo de quince días . . ." Leopoldo Alas, *loc. cit.*

which is just at the freezing point, is changed by the slightest concussion into ice."[5] In another place he tells us that when such a moment of intuition had brought him the over-all vision of a work, he then considered it as already created and looked on the task of writing it down as the work more of the artisan than the artist.[6]

Galdós' experience in the Puerta del Sol was, I believe, a moment of crystallization when his intuition revealed to him the relationships between many seemingly unrelated data filed away in his memory and showed him a pattern for presenting them in artistic form. I do not believe, despite the critics' many eulogies of *Gloria*, that Galdós had yet attained absolute mastery of his art, and consequently I think that the seams and joints between the various elements that Galdós brought together in *Gloria* are much more visible than in such a masterpiece as *Fortunata y Jacinta*. It is therefore advisable to begin an inquiry into Galdós' creative process by the study of just such a work as *Gloria*, where the chances of isolating the component elements are much greater.

But many could well question my fundamental hypothesis: "Why do you assume, because Coleridge and Goethe's minds worked in a certain way, that Galdós was also subject to the same mental process?" My argument, thus far, is of course analogical. But there are dozens of ways to substantiate the hypothesis which will come out in the course of this study. To anticipate a little, the very theme of the novel – the fundamental nobility of religion opposed to the narrow fanaticism of individual sects, which, instead of uniting men into one universal brotherhood, breed hate and division – this theme, I say, could scarcely have drifted into Galdós' mind out of mere nothing. The theme was hotly discussed in the University, the Ateneo, and the Congreso just before *Gloria* was composed. It was natural that it should remind Galdós of a French novel on a similar religious subject and of a family he had met only the summer before in which the

[5] Lowes, *op. cit.*, p. 148.

[6] This is told by U. González Serrano, "El naturalismo artístico," in *Cuestiones contemporáneas*, Madrid, 1883.

religious problem was important, as well as that it should bring to the surface many bits of earlier reading on religion. All these matters I shall treat at length later on in this chapter.

But the most obvious, although perhaps the least significant, sphere in which Galdós fused a quantity of his own observations to create an imaginary new reality is the sphere of topography. That is why I shall begin with a study of the setting of *Gloria*.

TOPOGRAPHY

On the first page of *Gloria*, Galdós tells us not to look for Ficóbriga on the map of Spain, as it exists only on the *mapa moral* of the country.[7] This statement can be paraphrased as follows: Ficóbriga is not a real town, although of course it must be made up (as will be shown) from elements of real towns, these elements chosen to produce one dominant emotional impression (which is *moral* in the broad Spanish meaning of the word).

Not long after the publication of the novel, Menéndez Pelayo asserted that Ficóbriga seems to be Castro Urdiales (near Santander).[8] As a matter of fact there are many points of resemblance. Both are seaports on the north coast, built on headlands which break abruptly into the sea. Each has a church, a cemetery, and a castle at the end of its point. The bay formed by the headland and a line of rocks projecting from it makes in each case a harbor, poorly protected but deep enough to permit small steamboats to load ore from nearby mines. Behind the towns, mountains rise not far from the ocean. Finally the ancient name of Castro Urdiales was "Flaviobriga,"[9] which resembles the name "Ficóbriga." All considered, I believe that Galdós must have used Castro Urdiales as his chief model for Ficóbriga in the first chapters of *Gloria*.

[7] *Gloria*, p. 499 (Pt. I, Chap. 1). The page citations from *Gloria* are always from Vol. IV of the *Obras completas*, Aguilar, S.A., Madrid, 1949. In each case I have added in parenthesis the part and chapter, to aid those who use other editions.

[8] *Historia de los heterodoxos españoles*, ed. Artigas, VII, 487.

[9] See Amós de Escalante, *Costas y montañas*, Madrid, 1871, pp. 27 and 48; also *Enciclopedia universal*, Espasa, XII, 408.

But besides the similarities between the two cities we must list a considerable number of dissimilarities. These are mostly of nomenclature – names of streets, mountains, rocky promontories, and so forth. In actual topography the one great difference is in the nature of the harbor, which is of great importance to us because it is the scene of the shipwreck, and this wreck forces Galdós to vary his plan of Ficóbriga as conceived in the early pages of the novel. In them the *ría* (a tidal estuary at the mouth of a river) emptying into the bay is described as navigable for small steamships; later Galdós states that the steamer *Plantagenet*, although it carries only eight men, one of whom is a passenger, is too big to enter the *ría*. The reasons for this change I shall investigate later; for the moment let me state that Castro Urdiales has only a tiny river or large stream, completely unnavigable, emptying into its bay.

Did Galdós know Castro Urdiales? He went to Santander for the first time in the summer of 1871 and was so impressed with the beauties of la Montaña that he returned every summer. As a souvenir of his first visit there is in his private library a copy of Juan García, *Costas y montañas* (Madrid, 1871), dedicated to Galdós as follows: "Para recuerdo de su visita a las costas y montañas cántabras, su amigo y compañero. Amós de Escalante. Santander, 28 de agosto 1871." This was not the only literary friendship which Galdós made at this time. We have his own account of his meeting with Pereda and the beginning of their long relationship.[10]

Early in 1872 the newspaper *El Debate* carried reviews of Pereda's *Tipos y paisajes* (January 26) and of Juan García's *Costas y montañas* (February 7). Although these reviews were unsigned, I believe they were the work of Galdós. In the first place Galdós was closely connected with *El Debate*, of which he was the editor from its foundation on January 16, 1871 to October 7, 1871. After giving up this position he still published in its

[10] This is given in the "Prólogo" of *El sabor de la tierruca* (1882), which was republished in Galdós, *Obras completas*, Aguilar, Madrid, 1942, VI, 1487.

columns. For example, his novel *La Sombra* ran serially from December 5 to December 26, 1871. On April 23, 1872, when a whole page was devoted to Cervantes, the leading article, although unsigned, was the same essay which appeared over Galdós' signature in *Las Cortes* (April 23, 1869), in *La Nación* (April 24, 1868) and in *Vida Nueva* (October 30 and November 6, 1898).

Then in Galdós' prologue to Pereda's *El sabor de la tierruca* (1882), he tells us that when he read the *Tipos y paisajes* in 1871 he was deeply impressed and because of this profound admiration visited Santander for the first time.[11] This corresponds to the statement of the reviewer in *El Debate*, who says that Pereda's work has awakened the public's interest in la Montaña, and who then talks from personal experience of its delights, showing clearly that he had been there recently for the first time. He promises a review of *Costas y montañas* in the near future. This second article reveals the fact that Juan García is a pseudonym for Amós de Escalante and that the reviewer knows well the picturesque beauty of la Montaña.

Now, in this second article Galdós (if you will concede that he is the reviewer)[12] describes the beauty of la Montaña, not basing his remarks on Escalante's work but on his own observation. Among other attractions of the province he cites the "alegres villas de Castro Urdiales, Laredo, Comillas y San Vicente de la Barquera," bathed by the northern sea. As he turns to Escalante's book, he informs us that Escalante begins his excursion at Castro Urdiales and describes minutely "esta interesantísima villa." I cannot feel that this epithet is based on Escalante's long (over 75 pages), diffuse, and to me boring description of the town. Rather it seems that both descriptive adjectives are the result of personal recollection.

[11] *Ibid.*

[12] Since writing the above I have found the following confirmation: ". . . lo que llenó de gozo a Pereda fué el artículo aparecido en *El Debate* (7-II-72), sin firma, pero escrito por Galdós . . ." (José M. de Cossío, *La obra literaria de Pereda*, pp. 68–69). Cossío confused the dates of the two articles in *El Debate*; Jean Camp (*José María de Pereda*, Paris, 1937, p. 24) compounds the confusion by misquoting the date as "7.11.71."

If this surmise is true, then Galdós knew Castro Urdiales as early as the summer of 1871. That he revisited the seaport in other excursions is also a distinct possibility. In his library is a guide book (published after *Gloria*) in which he marked heavily the route Santander – Castro Urdiales – Bilbao, showing that even after the writing of *Gloria* he still enjoyed travel along this stretch of coast. Although we cannot state with absolute certainty that Galdós had visited Castro Urdiales before writing *Gloria*, we can be sure that he knew enough about the town from his friend Amós de Escalante's book to have used it as the model of Ficóbriga. Yet I am left with the impression that he knew the town directly. Galdós' love of travel is well known. He probably took many excursions to towns around Santander similar to the one which we shall now consider in the attempt to explain the discrepancies in detail between Ficóbriga and the ancient Flaviobriga.

In the summer of 1876, at the invitation and in the company of Pereda, Galdós traveled through the western part of the Province of Santander. On his return, at the urging of his Cantabrian friends he wrote *Cuarenta leguas por Cantabria*, an account of the expedition for publication in their local literary review, *La Tertulia*. The work was printed in installments over the period from November 1876 to January 1877, and before the completion of this edition it appeared again in *La Revista de España* (November 28–December 28, 1876).[13] For us the importance of this article is that it gives us some of Galdós' impressions of the north coast from the months immediately preceding the composition of *Gloria*. If for his novel he borrowed features and names from other parts of la Montaña, amalgamating all of his recollections, those of recent months would naturally be the most vivid ones.

The church of Castro Urdiales, called "la parroquia de Santa María," has no special standing but is a mere parish church. Yet Galdós constantly calls the church of Ficóbriga "la abadía." This change takes us back to his recent experiences reflected in *Cuarenta leguas por Cantabria*. He begins this travelogue with

[13] Later part of it appeared in the *Revista Portorriqueña*, Vol. I (1888).

a description of Santillana del Mar and devotes one whole section to its famous abbey and another to its outstanding feature, the cloister.

Both the town and the church produce a sad feeling of decay. Entering the abbey through the atrium, one discovers a romanesque interior with some "arcos . . . peraltados,"[14] as if the building were aspiring to the Gothic. The observer's disenchantment arises not only from the dilapidated condition of the structure but principally from the heavy coat of plaster which covers everything, especially the renowned sculpture of the capitals and cornices. "Todo está cubierto y velado por una capa espesa de yeso; las figuras se ven como si estuvieran *arrebujadas en un manto blanco, bajo el cual tiemblan de frío* y de vergüenza."[15] Galdós notes the inclining columns in the cloister and the sorry condition of the whole.[16]

Now the church of Castro Urdiales is unusually poor in ornamental sculpture and has not, as far as I can tell, ever been plastered. Yet when Gloria observes the architecture of the old romanesque church of Ficóbriga, she notices that "estaba toda cubierta profanamente por una capa de yeso, bajo la cual las emblemáticas figurillas de los capiteles y de las archivoltas apenas tenían forma. Parecían *tiritar de frío arrebujadas en gruesos mantos blancos*. Algunos arcos ojivos o peraltados habían perdido, con el peso de tantos años, su original curva . . . algunas columnas habían dejado de ser verticales . . . El conjunto estético de tal fábrica era triste."[17]

The general similarities of these two descriptions would lead to no positive conclusion were it not for the metaphor repeated almost word for word. But with this verbal repetition it becomes obvious that Galdós was fusing impressions. From Castro Urdiales he took the imposing situation of the church of Santa María on its headland over the sea but changed its uninteresting interior for

[14] *Obras completas*, Aguilar, VI, 1495.
[15] *Ibid.*, p. 1496.
[16] *Ibid.*
[17] *Gloria*, p. 521 (I, 14).

that of the "abadía" of Santillana, which despite its plaster is unusually fine.[18]

In descriptions of the Ficobrigan abbey in later chapters of the novel, Galdós still has Santillana in mind. Once again he refers to the plastered interior, speaking of "aquellas piedras bárbaramente blanqueadas."[19] He talks of the atrium of the church and tells us that the Lantiguas' chapel "estaba en la derecha nave de la Abadía, con ventana ojiva abierta al atrio . . ."[20] At Castro Urdiales there is no atrium, but at Santillana this courtyard exists and is noted in Galdós' description. It does not have the usual location before the main doors opposite the apse, but is on the right side of the church, which is itself exceptional in having no doors at the end of the nave opposite the altar. Thus when one enters the door, one finds a chapel or two on the right side with windows opening onto the atrium. Such an arrangement could be possible only in a very limited number of churches which alter the traditional plan of ecclesiastical architecture, of which Santillana is one.

As Gloria and her aunt sit in the church awaiting the return of a religious procession, they hear shouts in the "plaza" outside.[21] Again Galdós must be thinking of Santillana, as it does have a square outside whereas the Castro Urdiales church stands in the midst of a small meadow. On a later page of the novel, this meadow surrounding the church and the adjacent cemetery is mentioned.[22] Although this is a mere detail, it tends to confirm my contention that Galdós has not reached his full artistic powers and sometimes juxtaposes, rather than fuses, his material. Obviously, the church could not have both a square and a meadow outside its doors.

The church of Ficóbriga dominates the town. Its tower is visible from a distance, and from some of the nearby valleys it is the only building of the town which can be seen.[23] This tower

[18] The abbey has since been restored and the plaster removed.
[19] *Gloria*, p. 558 (I, 29).
[20] *Ibid.*, 590 (II, 4). The atrium is mentioned earlier, *ibid.*, 571 (I, 35).
[21] *Ibid.*, 601 (II, 7).
[22] *Ibid.*, 625 (II, 15).
[23] *Ibid.*, 547 (I, 25).

is unfinished, "semejante a una cabeza sin sombrero; pero tiene en su campanario dos ojos vigilantes . . ."[24] It is true that in Castro Urdiales the church also dominates the town from its hill, but the unfinished tower hardly rises above the level of the roof and is not an imposing feature.[25] Its two windows, one above the other on each side, could not give the impression of eyes.

The tower of Santillana del Mar corresponds more exactly to Galdós' description of Ficóbriga. It rises well above the abbey and far over any other building of the town. It is unfinished in the sense that it does not have a steeple which would be like a hat upon a head. On three of its four sides it has double romanesque windows which could be likened to two eyes.[26] It is curious to see that this comparison to a head was not noted by Galdós in his travel description of Santillana. He mentions only the similarity of the church tower to *mozárabe* towers in Castile and finds that it gives an impression of austerity.[27] His imagination seems to have freer reign in the novel than in the more factual account.

One of the prominent features of the Abadía de Santillana is an ancient tomb, according to tradition that of the Infanta Fronilde.[28] No such tomb appears in the church of Ficóbriga. But Galdós did not forget the Infanta. When he wants to name a hill near Ficóbriga he calls it "la cotera de Fronilde."[29] "Cotera" is a local word of the Province of Santander indicating a steep-sided hill; "Fronilde" is a striking medieval name attached in Galdós' mind to a building about which he was constantly thinking as he created *Gloria*. In the second part of the novel he alters the

[24] *Ibid.*, 499 (I, 1).

[25] A picture showing the church is available in the *Enciclopedia Universal*, Espasa, XII, 409. Other good pictures can be seen in R. Amador de los Ríos, *Santander*, pp. 553–563; and in J. Fresnedo de la Calzada, *Santander y su provincia*, p. 220.

[26] See the photograph in V. Lampérez' *Historia de la arquitectura cristiana española*, I, 550. The tower is described in the text as follows: "La belleza de ésta se encuentra en el exterior; es cuadrada, y los cuatro muros están formados por una arquería ciega en la zona superior, y abierta con ventanas . . . en la inferior."

[27] *Obras completas*, Aguilar, VI, 1495.

[28] *Ibid.*, 1496.

[29] *Gloria*, 519 (I, 13).

name of the hill to "el cerro de Doña Fronilde." [30] Here the word "Doña" makes the allusion to the lady buried in Santillana more certain. There is little doubt about the origin of this name.

There is reason to believe that Santillana gradually superseded Castro Urdiales in Galdós' mind as the chief model for Ficóbriga. For example, his description of its houses in the early pages of *Gloria* emphasizes their squalor: "Las primeras casas . . . son miserables; las segundas también. . . . Las humildes casas estrechas y sucias no se caen al suelo por no dar qué decir . . ." [31] This corresponds accurately to Castro Urdiales. But twenty-two chapters later, when Daniel goes out to see the sights of the town, he examines with interest ". . . las casas infanzonas de la villa, algunas de las cuales llaman con justicia la atención de los forasteros." [32] Santillana, I hardly need point out, is a remarkably well preserved medieval town, noted not only for its abbey but also for several fine manorial houses. No such houses adorn the old part of Castro Urdiales.

The predominance of Santillana over Castro Urdiales shows up even more clearly in Galdós' allusions to Ficóbriga in *Marianela*, written a little over a year after *Gloria.* Again Galdós chooses a setting in Cantabria, specifically the mining village which he calls Socartes, whose model has been identified as Reocín,[33] not far from Torrelavega and about forty-five miles west of Castro Urdiales. Thus we are surprised to hear him say that an underground river at Socartes may join the sea near Ficóbriga,[34] that a distant view of the sea near Ficóbriga can be had from Socartes,[35] and that a rainbow, visible from the mining village, rests one foot on the Ficobrigan hills.[36] Obviously, if Socartes is Reocín, Ficóbriga is not, at this stage in Galdós' thought, the distant Castro Urdiales.

But an even greater surprise awaits us in *Marianela.* The heroine

[30] *Ibid.*, 590 (II, 3).
[31] *Ibid.*, 499 (I, 1).
[32] *Ibid.*, 541 (I, 23).
[33] J. Ortega Munilla in *El Imparcial,* Mar. 12, 1888.
[34] *Marianela, Obras completas,* Aguilar, IV, 687.
[35] *Ibid.*, 702.
[36] *Ibid.*, 746.

of the novel, wishing she could be a bird, says she would like to fly to the hill which is between Ficóbriga and the sea.[37] The novelist has forgotten that his city was a seaport! The Castro Urdiales element in Ficóbriga has given way completely to the Santillana component. The latter town does in fact have a hill between it and the sea, and its hills and the sea beyond them are indeed visible from Reocín.

Not only memories of Santillana and Castro Urdiales fused to make the composite which Galdós called Ficóbriga. He must have had a tremendous number of impressions of la Montaña which never appear in his literary works. Obviously he knew intimately the city of Santander and its surroundings and, I believe, drew from it some elements of Ficóbriga. In this imaginary city a line of rocks projects from the sea and partly shelters the harbor. Galdós calls them "Los Camellos." Now in Castro Urdiales there is such a line of rocks but they are called "el escollo de Santa Ana."[38] I questioned several fishermen of the town who knew no rocks or place called "Los Camellos" along the coast. But in Santander, at the beginning of the first beach of the Sardinero, some rocks called "Los Camellos" rise from the water.[39] Galdós saw them constantly during his various sojourns in the city. They do not help form a harbor and have no similarity to the "escollo de Santa Ana" other than rising from the water. Yet when the necessity of supplying a name for the rocks at Ficóbriga presented itself, this similarity was enough to bring about the change of names.

Ficóbriga is indebted to Santander for more than "Los Camellos." In the 1870s there was an extensive pine grove just behind the beaches of the Sardinero, a short distance west of the semisubmerged rocks. Galdós mentions it in *Amadeo I* where he describes Santander as he saw it in 1871 and 1872.[40] Ficóbriga also has its

[37] *Ibid.*, 702.

[38] Amós de Escalante, *Costas y montañas*, Renacimiento, Madrid, 1921, pp. 38–39.

[39] The map of Santander in *Enciclopedia universal*, Espasa, LIV, 208, calls the rocks "El camello" but the map given out by the National Tourist Office has the name in the plural.

[40] *Obras completas*, Aguilar, III, 1074–1075 (Chap. 22); see also Escalante, *op. cit.*, p. 193.

pine woods lying near the sea to the west of the city,[41] but Castro Urdiales does not and did not have any such forest. The road to the west hugs the coast, passing between the sea and the mountain of San Pelayo, which rises abruptly from the water.[42]

A few other details of Ficobrigan topography can be related to Galdós' real experiences in Cantabria. The tidal estuary, which twists and turns "como si no supiera a dónde dirigirse ni dónde está el mar que la espera . . ." [43] corresponds to numerous *rías* of the northern coast, some of which Galdós described in *Cuarenta leguas por Cantabria.* The river Nansa, for example, finding its way blocked by mountains "da dos o tres vueltas, como si meditara qué resolución debe tomar en presencia de tan grave apuro, y, al fin, por un boquete angosto descubre el mar." [44] But here the correspondence is not exact and the commonness of this geographical feature leads to the conclusion that Galdós had no one model in mind.

In *Gloria* we also have a hotel kept by a Frenchman,[45] perhaps a reminiscence of a hotel, also run by a Frenchman, in which Galdós passed a night on his trip with Pereda.[46] We discover, too, that Ficóbriga is beginning to attract summer visitors for the sea bathing, which was in fact true of Castro Urdiales.[47] None of these similarities is sufficiently precise, however, to constitute proof that the novelist used these specific details as models for the corresponding details of his fictional work.

Once we see that Ficóbriga is a composite of Castro Urdiales, Santillana, and Santander, with a few vaguer elements which could come from many places in the Province of Santander, we have accounted for almost all the topography of the imaginary city. Among the unexplained names, those of the streets "de la Poterna" and "del Cristo Viejo" were probably common in many

[41] *Gloria,* 553 (I, 28).
[42] Escalante, *op. cit.,* p. 47.
[43] *Gloria,* 499 (I, 1).
[44] *Obras completas,* Aguilar, VI, 1502.
[45] *Gloria,* 605 (II, 9).
[46] *Obras completas,* Aguilar, VI, 1502.
[47] The bathing house at Castro Urdiales was established in 1865. See *El Periódico Ilustrado,* II (1866), 194.

medieval cities. The towns near Ficóbriga—Villamojada (the nearest railway station) and Villamores where Gloria's child is hidden—bear purely imaginary names, similar in formation to Villahorrenda in *Doña Perfecta.* The mountain, Monteluz, and the square, la plazuela de la Charca, seem also to have fictitious names. There remain the two meadows "la Pesqueruela" and "Rebenque," the bridge "de Judas,"[48] and the "soto de Briján" whose names seem not to be invented. The Lantigua mansion, composed of an old and a new portion, is so particularized and removed from the conventional pattern as to make me think that Galdós had some specific model in mind, but which I do not know.[49]

From what we now know of the physical make-up of Ficóbriga we can derive two principles which apply to all of Galdós' creative process. Just as he fused geography here, so is there a similar trend to amalgamate elements of plot, character, and philosophy. And as one element of the geographical composite may temporarily take precedence over the others in the author's mind, in the same way he will stress now one, now another, of the components which constitute the raw material of his plot and characters.

THE *AMBIENTE MORAL*

Ficóbriga, formed of recollections of la Montaña, does not have a real existence, but its atmosphere is real. It exists not on the *mapa político* but on the *mapa moral*; its tone, its emotional atmosphere, is true to life. It is a little city inhabited by people like the Lantigua family—pleasant, helpful, courteous people whose only blemish is that they are intolerant in religion. They belong to the reactionary (*neocatólico*) group which yearns for

[48] This bridge resembles the one at Comillas, described by Galdós in *Cuarenta leguas por Cantabria* (*Obras completas,* VI, 1498).

[49] Galdós visited the mansion of the Marqués de Casa-Mena at the edge of Santillana (see *Obras completas,* VI, 1497). The mansion was the possession of one of the literary men who contributed to *La Tertulia,* one whom Galdós mentions in *Cuarenta leguas.* This house, partly restored and partly ancient, may have suggested the Lantigua home, for, as shown above, the houses of Santillana entered Galdós' concept of Ficóbriga.

the good old days of the absolute monarch and all-powerful church, which sees in liberalism and progress a force which will stifle virtue and undermine the patriarchal simplicity of Spanish life. At times their abhorrence of liberalism will even lead them to take arms for Don Carlos (the absolutist Pretender). But in their dealings with you, you will find them thoughtful, generous, and well mannered.

Don Juan de Lantigua, Gloria's father, is just such a person. A man of intelligence and imagination, imbued with admiration for the Spanish *Siglo de Oro*, he comes to believe that religion is not only the guide and director of the individual's conscience, but also a kind of official instrument to police all human activities.[50] In this he reveals the typical neo-Catholic attitude. However, when these ideas are not directly involved, Don Juan is the most charming companion. "En la vida práctica, Lantigua transigía benignamente con los hombres de ideas más contrarias a las suyas, y aun se le conocieron amigos íntimos, a los cuales amó mucho, pero sin poderles convencer nunca. En la vida de las ideas era donde campeaba su intransigencia y aquella esterilidad de roca jamás conmovida de su asiento por nada ni por nadie." [51] We shall soon see that this characterization of Don Juan de Lantigua could easily be used to describe Galdós' principal literary friends in Santander.

Clarín praises his friend Galdós precisely because he has drawn such a tolerant picture of Spanish intolerance in *Gloria.* Yet Galdós had just given us another picture of fanaticism in *Doña Perfecta*; there he did not restrain himself but let his deep-seated hatred of intolerance color his portraits of Perfecta and the Penitenciario, who are treacherous and villainous almost beyond the point of verisimilitude. What accounts for the author's changed attitude toward the neo-Catholics in the second novel?

When thinking of the Cantabrian coast, Galdós did not think

[50] *Gloria*, 504 (I, 4).

[51] *Ibid.* Compare what Galdós says of his discussions of politics and religion with Pereda, in which "Pereda no cedía nunca." *Discursos leídos ante la Real Academia Española en las recepciones públicas del 7 y 21 de febrero de 1897*, Madrid, 1897, p. 153.

of people of a darkly reactionary character. His friends in the north were men like Amós de Escalante, Menéndez Pelayo, and Pereda. The first was modest, a great lover of solitude and of nature, equally enamored of his native province and with the glorious Spain of the sixteenth century.[52] A traditionalist indeed, whose novel *Ave Maris Stella* (1877) catches the style and feeling of the mystic writers of the Golden Age, but a poetic traditionalist sentimentally attached to a romanticized past, he has points of similarity with Don Cayetano Polentinos, at whom Galdós smiled in *Doña Perfecta.*

Galdós met the seventeen-year-old prodigy Marcelino Menéndez Pelayo in 1873.[53] This puritanical stripling passed a stern judgment on his friend and especially on *Gloria* four years after the publication of the novel. Galdós is for him "el enemigo implacable y frío del catolicismo," although he is also an "hombre dulce y honrado."[54] It is only fair to state that his bitterness mellowed greatly with time, so that in 1897 he can say of *Gloria* and *La familia de León Roch*: "Yo mismo, en los hervores de mi juventud, los ataqué con violenta saña, sin que por eso mi íntima amistad con el señor Galdós sufriese la menor quiebra."[55] Although his first opinion was that the characters of *Gloria* were unfair and exaggerated, he comes to believe later that Galdós has given them "condiciones nobilísimas," although along with high qualities he has endowed them with "el germen de lo que él llama intolerancia."[56]

Pereda also found in Pérez Galdós a man whose personal character charmed and won him but whose liberalism and tolerance puzzled and pained him. The long letters which Pereda wrote to

[52] See M. Menéndez Pelayo, *Estudios* (Cuarta serie), in *Obras completas*, Artigas, XI, 281ff.

[53] On Feb. 7, 1897, Menéndez Pelayo stated "Más de veintitrés años hace . . . tuve la honra de estrechar relaciones de amistad [con Galdós]." See *Discursos*, p. 33.

[54] Menéndez Pelayo, *Historia de los heterodoxos en España*, ed. Artigas, VII, 486–487. In Galdós' library there is a copy of Menéndez Pelayo's *Epístola a mis amigos de Santander*, Madrid, 1879, with the following dedication: "A mi amigo el eminente (aunque heterodoxo) novelista D. Benito Pérez Galdós. M. Menéndez Pelayo."

[55] M. Pelayo, *Discursos . . . R. Academia*, p. 72.

[56] *Ibid.*, p. 73.

Galdós after the publication of *Gloria* can be taken as a sample of his feeling, as can *De tal palo, tal astilla* (Pereda's answer to *Gloria*).[57]

If Galdós' friends in Santander reacted in this way to him and to his *Gloria*, how did he judge them? He found in them persons of charm, literary taste, and good breeding. As early as January 1872, after his first trip to Cantabria, he lists among the advantages of the region "la sensatez y rectitud de sus habitantes, el carácter hospitalario de su capital . . ." [58] Just before the writing of *Gloria* he speaks of his "cariñosos amigos montañeses" and singles out Amós de Escalante and Pereda for special mention.[59] Menéndez Pelayo and a number of other regular contributors to *La Tertulia* are also named less prominently. His friendship with Pereda, despite their arguments over religion and politics, is warmly remembered in both the prologue of *El sabor de la tierruca* (1882) and the *Memorias de un desmemoriado* (1905).[60] In 1897 Menéndez Pelayo sponsored Galdós' entrance into the Academia de la lengua and the latter served Pereda in like capacity.

Surely the Santander men were among Galdós' best and most steadfast friends. But always there remained the germ of intolerance, which was particularly noticeable in 1876. Young Menéndez Pelayo was embroiled in polemics with Azcárate, Revilla, and Salmerón, showing himself a bitter enemy of progress and modern philosophical trends.[61] Pereda had been *diputado* of the Carlist cause; he had fought against freedom of religion in the Cortes.[62] He approved of Menéndez Pelayo's attacks against the philosophers, calling him "el azote de la farsa alemanesca" [63] and,

[57] The letters are printed by Cossío, *op. cit.*, pp. 130–151.

[58] *El Debate*, Jan. 26, 1872.

[59] *Cuarenta leguas*, in *Obras completas*, Aguilar, VI, 1507.

[60] *Obras completas*, Aguilar, VI, 1488 and 1736.

[61] See L. A. de Olmet y A. García Carraffa, *Menéndez Pelayo*, Madrid, 1913, pp. 31 and 52–53. In 1876 Menéndez Pelayo published the plan of his *Heterodoxos españoles* in the *Revista Europea*, VIII, revealing his deep antagonism to *krausimo* and modern philosophical trends.

[62] Boris de Tannenberg, in *Revue Hispanique*, V (1898), 339.

[63] See J. M. Cossío, *Obras completas de Pereda*, Estudio preliminar, Aguilar, p. 24.

what is more, he even wrote (probably at Menéndez' instigation and certainly with his most hearty approval) a satire on the *krausistas* called "El Sabio" (published in *Tipos trashumantes*, 1877).[64] These were models of Don Juan de Lantigua's spirit and in general of the *ambiente moral* of Ficóbriga.

Galdós' attitude toward his Cantabrian friends must have been very similar to Valera's. The latter sustained a lifelong friendship and correspondence with Menéndez Pelayo, although in politics and religion he held very different views.[65] Valera, without losing Menéndez Pelayo's esteem, can chide him on his *neocatolicismo* in vigorous terms.[66] Yet, when all is said and done, the *neocatólicos*, says Valera, are the most pleasant people to associate with. Making allowance for Valera's marked aristocratic leanings, I believe we have in his attitude one comparable to that of Galdós.

There is still another human factor which drew Galdós' attention to the religious problem as manifested in Santander. When he was summering there with his two sisters in 1876, he met a family which epitomized the solution of conflicts of faith. In his boarding house lived a Mr. Lund, a Norwegian Protestant who had lived many years in Bilbao and had married a Vizcayan Catholic woman. Because of Spanish intolerance, it was impossible for the two to marry in Spain but they circumvented this obstacle by going to Bordeaux for the ceremony. Now their

[64] In a review of *Tipos trashumantes* in *La Tertulia*, Vol. II, Menéndez states that Pereda has not taken his *sabio*'s speech from maniacs but from the gravest Spanish philosophers.

[65] *Epistolario de Valera y Menéndez Pelayo*, Madrid, 1946, p. 102: "¿Por qué seré yo, siendo tan liberalote, tan neocatólico en la amistad?"; p. 188: "¿Por qué ha de hacerse liberal toda la gente soez y bellaca?"; see also pp. 322 and 406.

[66] In a review of Menéndez Pelayo's *Heterodoxos* Valera notes that the former identifies being Catholic with being what is commonly called neo-Catholic. He protests as follows: "Diré sólo que, si es menester sostener para ser buen católico, que la religión debe imponerse por fuerza; que la Inquisición es o fué digna de elogio; que la libertad de pensamiento, de imprenta y de cultos es mala; y que es abominable el parlamentarismo . . . yo soy un católico malo y sospechoso. En suma, yo no creo que el ser católico implique ser carlista, o por lo menos, absolutista." (From J. Valera, *Obras completas*, XXV, 109–110.) The attitude Valera denounces is that of the youthful Menéndez Pelayo, and, by extension, of all neo-Catholics.

happy marriage was symbolized for Galdós in an eighteen-year-old daughter, Juanita, in whom some critics have seen the model of Gloria.[67]

Leaving the question of models until later, I wish here to stress the importance of the Lund family in the creation of *Gloria*. The attitude of Galdós' other northern friends stands in sharp contrast to the religious tolerance which made this family possible. Now the significant thing is that his contact with the charming but intolerant neo-Catholics did not inspire a novel until they were contrasted in his mind with a couple who had found in love the solution to the conflict of religions. In the novel *Gloria* love also is the solution to conflicting faiths but this time it does not triumph. The intolerance of both Catholicism and Judaism (and, by extension, of all established cults) works to undo that which nature has wrought and God himself has ordained. If only the Santander people could lose the germ of intolerance; if only they could become Catholic instead of neo-Catholic, remembering the divine command: "Love ye one another!" This thought was in Galdós' mind, consciously or subconsciously, as he directed his steps toward the Café Universal in December 1876.

RELIGION AND RELIGIONS

Galdós, as a boy, lived under neo-Catholic religious influences. His stern, puritanical, intolerant mother (who was later his chief model for Doña Perfecta[68]) caused him to distrust uncharitable religiosity. Then as a youthful student in Madrid, Benito came

[67] I owe the facts set forth here and later to the kindness of Doña Juana Lund de Achúcarro herself. I had the pleasure of meeting her in March 1951 through the courtesy of Dr. Gregorio Marañón. At the age of 93 she was still very bright and active. She remembered that she met Galdós in the summer after the end of the Carlist War (1876). She and her parents happened to live in the same hotel or boarding house as Galdós. Juana became a very close friend of Galdós' sisters, of whom she spoke in the highest terms of praise.

Juana's parents lived in Bilbao and there she passed almost all her life. She married Sr. Achúcarro, a doctor, at 21. Because her husband did not like to travel she seldom left the city. She never saw San Quintín, Galdós' summer home in Santander. Only occasionally did she take a trip to Madrid.

[68] Berkowitz, *Pérez Galdós*, p. 19.

under wholly different religious influences. About ten years before his arrival, a new philosophy, Krausism, had taken hold in Madrid. Besides being a philosophy (or rational explanation of the universe), Krausism had appeals above and beyond the purely intellectual ones. It called on men to live nobly and simply, dedicating their lives to the service and enlightenment of their fellows; it held out hopes of social reforms and a betterment of man's terrestial lot; it concerned itself above all with religion, advocating a pruning from existing religions of man-made rules with a corresponding return to the essential religious spirit, fundamentally the same in all cults. Thus tolerance was one of its cardinal beliefs.[69]

Krausismo at first existed only among the intellectuals. Its founder, Sanz del Río, was a professor at the Universidad Central and had a number of followers (as well as enemies) among the professors and students. Galdós, whose active attendance at the University was limited to one year, came under the influence of *krausismo* in the person of Fernando de Castro, his teacher of history, about whom he wrote a laudatory essay.[70] Other younger *krausistas* from the University circle later became his friends, among them Clarín, Palacio Valdés, and Giner de los Ríos. These men's enthusiastic reviews of Galdós' early books bear witness to their admiration for him.[71]

The place in which these friendships were formed and fostered was not the University but the Ateneo. Here intellectuals of all persuasions could meet and argue for their particular beliefs. The "secciones" were given over to debate on previously fixed subjects. Not infrequently *krausismo* was attacked or defended. Galdós, although never taking part in the discussions, was certainly fully aware of the burning issue of the day. In later years,

[69] P. Jobit, *Les éducateurs de l'Espagne contemporaine – Les Krausistes,* Vol. I, gives a sympathetic and masterful picture of the movement. See especially Vol. I, Chap. 5, "Le Problème Religieux."

[70] Published in *La Nación,* Feb. 16, 1868, and in *Correo de España,* Feb. 13, 1871.

[71] Clarín's first writing on Galdós is his review of *Gloria* in the *Revista Europea,* 1877; Palacio Valdés dedicates two eulogistic articles to him in the *Revista Europea,* XI (1878); Giner reviewed *La fontana de oro* in the *Revista meridional,* 1871.

describing the Ateneo of his youth, he praises it as the place where "nació la Buena Nueva, y allí tuvo su laboriosa gestación, hasta dar al mundo hispano el fruto bendito de la democracia, del laicismo, de la tolerancia mínima . . ." [72] *La Buena Nueva* (note the Biblical origin of this phrase) was the lay religion of *krausismo*, or if we are not to accept so narrow an interpretation, it was at least the philosophic spirit, the spirit of rational examination of all truths, or *libre pensamiento*, which was fostered by *krausismo*.

To prove beyond question that Galdós felt the effects of this philosophic renaissance we have merely to examine his early journalistic output. Between 1865 and 1873 he contributed to eight different periodicals, most of them organs of the *progresista* party, which was the militant arm of the *krausista* movement. Let us examine the over-all tone of some of these papers.[73] *Las Novedades* describes itself as "un órgano incansable del partido liberal; un adalid del progreso en sus diversas manifestaciones sociales, políticas, científicas, artísticas y literarias; un periódico consagrado a la defensa de todas las aplicaciones sinceras de los principios constitucionales." [74] In the same issue it states: "El partido progresista nos cuenta como hijos suyos . . ." and throughout its run it contains numerous articles against the *neocatólicos*, the irreconcilable enemies of the *krausistas* and the *progresistas*. This, then, is a typical example of the kind of papers on which Galdós worked and for whose program he must have felt sympathy.

Three of the periodicals to which he contributed—*El Contemporáneo*, *El Debate*, and *La Revista de España*—were the property of the same man, José Luis Albareda. Galdós had a respectful admiration for Albareda, whom he called one of his masters in journalism. Galdós would not have looked up to Albareda, nor would the latter have chosen the former to be editor of the last two of these three periodicals, had they not

[72] See "Guía espiritual de España," in *Obras completas*, Aguilar, VI, 1560.

[73] No thorough examination of Galdós' journalistic career has yet been made. I hope to present my findings on the subject in the near future.

[74] Issue of Jan. 7, 1868.

shared almost identical views on politics and religion. Albareda was a believer in complete religious freedom and an enthusiastic supporter of self-government, but within the framework of a constitutional monarchy.[75] Thus *El Debate* supports the rule of Amadeo I, in spite of the growing agitation for a republic. At the same time it is wholly in favor of the modern spirit and material progress while condemning roundly the "brutal intolerancia" and the subjection of state to church characteristic of the last years of Isabel II's rule.[76]

This is enough, I believe, to show the general tone of liberalism which infused the atmosphere that young Benito Pérez Galdós inhaled. The specific articles from his pen reveal an attitude of cautious liberalism in politics and an out-and-out hatred of fanaticism and intolerance in religion. His attacks on the *neos* (as the neo-Catholics were derisively called) are frequent and savage.[77]

Just as Galdós supported the applied *krausismo* of the *progresista* party before the Revolution of 1868, so he championed its program in the Cortes Constituyentes after the revolution. Spain suddenly found itself transported from reactionary traditionalism to the most modern progressive conditions. In the Cortes, where for the first time since the Middle Ages, freedom of religion was established in Spain, *krausista* orators talked in favor of a new, more inclusive faith, so broad that all could commune within it. Young Galdós thrilled to these ideas as he covered the sessions of the Cortes for his newspaper.[78]

[75] There is a valuable article on Albareda by A. Linares Rivas in *El Constitucional*, May 14, 1878. See also *Les Matinées Espagnoles*, I (1886), pp. 33 and 61; and *La Ilustracion de Madrid*, II (1871), 359–362 (with a portrait of Albareda on p. 357).

[76] See the leading article of the first issue, Jan. 16, 1871.

[77] His attacks on the *neos* were so common that he ends one article (in *La Nación*, Feb. 2, 1868) with the words: "Demos punto final. Antes os pido un voto de gracias. He escrito una Revista y no he hablado de los *neos*."

[78] He wrote a column called "Crónica parlamentaria" in the newspaper *Las Cortes*. In his *Memorias* (*Obras completas*, VI, 1734) he recalls ". . . el ruido de las Constituyentes, palabras desgranadas del famoso discurso de Castelar contra Manterola, cláusulas de Figueras, apóstrofes de Fernando Garrido, de Paúl y Angulo, estridencias lejanas de gritos y aplausos . . ." Castelar thundered against the narrow concept of God ("Grande es el

The situation was further complicated by the quarrel between the newly united Italian state and the papacy. The Spanish liberals were generally in favor of the state over the church, especially when Pio IX took an intransigent stand in the *Syllabus* against all that liberalism stood for. Naturally the Spanish traditionalists supported the pope, and were firmly opposed to Amadeo I as King of Spain. After all, was he not the son of the impious Victor Immanuel who was keeping His Holiness a prisoner in the Vatican? At this time, let us remember, Galdós was editor of a newspaper (*El Debate*) whose whole policy centered around support of King Amadeo.

What were the actions of the neo-Catholic opponents of *krausismo*? In a general way they supported the absolute monarchy and all-powerful church. But specifically they fought *krausismo* by driving the *krausista* professors from their chairs with accusations of broken censorship rules. Even Menéndez Pelayo, himself a professor, spoke warmly in the congress against academic freedom and in favor of the governmental dismissal of the *krausista* professors.[79] So consistent was their antagonism to philosophy or any rational examination of accepted ideas that Donoso Cortés, a neo-Catholic of the preceding generation, went to the extreme of denying that reason can teach us anything, a doctrine which the church itself condemned. They sought out heretical aspects of *krausismo* in the hope of having it anathematized; they glorified the philosophies of the past in the belief that young men would find in them a substitute for the fascinating modern doctrine.

Dios en el Sinaí . . ."), upholding in its stead the idea of a tolerant God of loving-kindness. Figueras was the chief of the republican party, later (1873) president of the First Spanish Republic. Garrido supported the international labor movement, then considered a menace to property, religion, and the family; he also declared Catholicism dead. Paúl y Angulo was a rather crude and brutal leader of the common people. All these men figure prominently in the last series of *Episodios Nacionales*. Their speeches can be read in the *Diario de las sesiones*, 1869–1871 (esp. Vol. III).

[79] His speech, the only one he ever made as a *diputado*, ends, "Para mí, la frase libertad de la ciencia, ni en el terreno filosófico, ni en el terreno legal, ni en el terreno histórico, puede racionalmente legitimarse." See Olmet y Carraffa, *Menéndez Pelayo*, p. 94.

Although tolerance is fundamental in *krausista* religious reform, the new philosophers could scarcely love the neo-Catholics. They found particularly irksome the traditionalists' refusal to take philosophy – any philosophy – seriously. But not all Catholics in Spain were neo-Catholics, and with the others the *krausistas* got along splendidly. They admired Balmes, a philosopher and priest of the preceding generation; they extolled Fray Zeferino González, Bishop of Córdoba, who at least discussed and challenged their system on rational grounds.[80] They even had supporters among the liberal clergy, especially in a group of priests who founded a newspaper called *La Armonía* and set out to undo the work of the traditionalists.[81]

Just what were the religious forms of *krausismo*, and do they manifest themselves in *Gloria*? A fundamental assumption which underlies the whole philosophy is that a historical law exists, applicable to all beings and activities, each one of which is in the

[80] See G. de Azcárate in *Revista de España*, LXX (1879), 175–176.

[81] Galdós' newspaper, *El Debate*, announces the new collaborator in these terms: "*La Armonía*, periódico redactado por sacerdotes, pone de manifiesto el intransigente sistema de los diarios neo-católicos, órganos por lo general de los seglares, partidarios más o menos fanáticos del absolutismo histórico y de la supremacía del poder de la Iglesia sobre todos los poderes. El citado periódico, que se blasona de ser el verdadero defensor de los intereses del catolicismo, pertenece a la escuela liberal con tanto éxito preconizada por célebres escritores católicos franceses y alemanes, y trata de combatir enérgicamente esa entrometida escuela irreconciliable, que tiene por adalides a unos cuantos seglares, poseídos de un rabioso celo por los intereses de la Iglesia, que están comprometiendo cada día. *La Armonía* dice a los diarios absolutistas lo siguiente:

"Porque os conocemos levantamos cruzada. Componemos la vanguardia de esa agrupación poderosa que se llama Iglesia. No nos vereis, como os hemos visto, empuñando el arma fratricida en varias intentonas a que apelásteis para probar fortuna; no nos vereis con el Cristo en la mano maldecir el progreso y las libertades públicas . . . Nos vereis, como nos ha visto siempre la sociedad, dignos sacerdotes . . . amantes del pueblo en que vivimos, del que procedemos, y al que deseamos la mayor ilustración, que sólo puede conseguir bajo la bandera de la libertad." (*El Debate*, Feb. 23, 1871). Compare to this Galdós' final comment on the neo-Catholic banquet and speeches in *Gloria*: "Mientras una docena de laicos arreglaban así, después de comer bien, los asuntos de la Iglesia católica . . ." (*Gloria*, p. 569; I, 34).

Menéndez Pelayo (*Heterodoxos*, ed. Artigas, VII, 441 and 469) alludes to the editors of *La Armonía*, accusing them of leaning toward heresies, such as Jansenism and the "Old Catholic" sect.

beginning a single idea or being, then falls into component parts opposed in some aspect to one another, and finally is synthesized into a harmonious whole.[82] Specifically in religion, the spirit is the same in all religions that are worthy of the name, but in historical development the various faiths have established rules which separate and oppose their communicants one to the other. The third stage, the harmonious amalgamation of all cults into one truly universal church remains to be accomplished in the future.[83] It cannot be achieved without a return to the original spirit of religion (essentially, the love of God and of one's fellow men), to accomplish which the existing sects must do away with man-made rules, separating the accidental from the essential. All dogmas and rituals are, therefore, subject to rational inquiry and may be abandoned if found wanting.

Some specific aspects of religious life which the *krausistas* condemned were asceticism, monastic seclusion, celibacy of the clergy, and persecution of dissenters. But all religions (as well as all philosophies) contain some truth. Although Christianity is the best existing religion, it does not embrace all the truth and is often overloaded with dogma which defeats the spirit of religion itself. The good *krausista* will respect all religions and show universal tolerance but he will examine all of them, accepting that which is in keeping with the spirit of religion and rejecting accidental accretions. He will use his reason in this examination, but in the final test he will appeal to his conscience, man's surest guide to what constitutes truly the spirit of religion. Each individual will dedicate himself to his own calling, remembering always that he is a part of humanity and striving always for the good and harmonious unification of all. Then ultimately a single state and a single church will replace the conflicting institutions of our days.

[82] See *Médula del sistema de Krause . . .*, comentado por G. Tiberghien, versión castellana de M. L., Madrid, 1874, p. 4.

[83] C. Ch. Krause, *Ideal de la humanidad para la vida, con introducción y comentarios por D. Julián Sanz del Río . . .*, Madrid, 1860, pp. 52–53, 74–76, and 236–249. See also the "universal church" aspired to by Fernando de Castro in his *Memoria testamentaria* (on which consult Jobit, *op. cit.*, I, 57, n. 3).

Now in *Gloria* the fundamental beliefs of both the Jew Daniel Morton and the Catholic Gloria Lantigua are identical. Their concept of God, which is another way of saying the spirit of their religion, is the same. But this essential part of religion has been submerged in a whole series of man-made rules. Gloria exclaims: "He aquí que ataja nuestros pasos y corta el hilo de vida que nos une, no Dios, autor de los corazones, de la virtud y el amor, sino los hombres, que con sus disputas, sus rencores, sus envidias, sus vanidades, han dividido las creencias, destruyendo la obra de Jesús, que a todos quiso reunirlos." [84]

Daniel explains to his mother that Judaism is to him narrow and insufficient. He can no longer worship the tribal god of the Chosen People. "No: yo adoro al Dios grande, al Jehová primitivo y augusto, al que dió los mandamientos, y desde entonces no dijo más porque no había más que decir; al que en su grandeza nos exige ofrendas de verdad, justicia y bondad, no formas de culto idolátrico; nos exige pensamientos, amor, acciones y esa mirada interna que purifica, no palabras rezadas, ni retahilas dichas de memoria." [85] The spirit of religion is noble and great; but religions, overladen with man's interpretations, have become mean and spiteful, dividing those whom they should, by definition, unite.

But if men have done this to religion men can undo it, as Gloria observes.[86] Perhaps, says Galdós, in the fullness of time, after many Glorias have succumbed, the spirit of religion will prevail.[87] In the meantime, we should aspire to the realization of this ideal. We can at least expect to find in heaven this all-embracing, new religion of the future.[88] In saying this, Galdós shows himself aware of the practical difficulties which beset idealism and which he expresses through Daniel's mother, Esther Spinoza.[89]

Both Gloria and Daniel examine their cults rationally and find

[84] *Gloria*, p. 551 (I, 26).
[85] *Ibid*., p. 657 (II, 28).
[86] *Ibid*., p. 554 (I, 28).
[87] *Ibid*., p. 677 (II, 33).
[88] *Ibid*., p. 678 (II, 33).
[89] *Ibid*., p. 658 (II, 28).

certain dogmas incomprehensible. Even as a girl Gloria began to use her intelligence to criticize literature, life, and religion, and although her father reprimanded her for her presumption, she still heard a secret voice telling her "Tu entendimiento es superior . . . levántate y piensa."[90] And think she did. For example, she cannot bring herself to believe in the existence of hell,[91] nor can she submit completely to the will of her Uncle Angel and Aunt Serafina who want her to renounce her child and become a nun.[92] Daniel also finds, as we have seen, shortcomings in his faith; witness, too, the fact that he dies insane searching for the new, all-embracing religion.

In addition to these critical expressions of his hero and heroine, Galdós also reveals his disapproval of mortification of the flesh, puritanism, and monasticism in his description of Doña Serafina.[93] This inhuman saint lived up to the letter of all man-made dogma but completely missed the God-given spirit of religion. Weak from fasting, she was capable of preparing her niece an ample breakfast without succumbing to the temptations of her abused body. She never deviated from her intention to force Gloria out of life and into a convent.

The ultimate court of appeal in matters of religion is the conscience. Daniel, pondering the difficulties of his situation, says to himself: "¿Qué pienso, qué creo yo? Conciencia, muéstrame lo que tienes más oculto, tu voz más recóndita; lo que es aún menos que voz, un susurro que apenas oigo yo mismo . . ."[94] Later he feels that God has spoken to him directly through a still, small voice and follows its dictates filled with a celestial joy.[95]

At the same time that Daniel invokes his conscience on his fundamental beliefs he asks himself "¿Qué creo yo? ¿Creo acaso que mi religión es la única en que los hombres pueden salvarse, la única que contiene verdades eternas? No: felizmente sé remontar mi espíritu por encima de todos los cultos, y puedo ver a

[90] *Ibid.*, p. 509 (I, 6).
[91] *Ibid.*, p. 577 (I, 37).
[92] *Ibid.*, p. 631 (II, 18).
[93] *Ibid.*, p. 640 (II, 21).
[94] *Ibid.*, p. 638 (II, 20).
[95] *Ibid.*, p. 656 (II, 28).

mi Dios, el Dios único, el grande, el terrible, el amoroso, el legislador, extendiéndose sobre todas las almas y presidiéndolas con la sonrisa de su bondad infinita desde el centro de toda substancia." [96] All religions have some of the eternal truths. They exist in Christianity although disfigured and adulterated. If it were not for the fact that Daniel's race had suffered centuries of persecution from the Christians, he could look upon them with perfect tolerance.

Just as Daniel sees good in all religions so does Gloria. Her uncle, the bishop, refuses her absolution for precisely this reason. She is, according to Don Angel, infected with *latitudinarianism.* She says to herself: "Los hombres pueden encontrar el camino de la eterna salvación y conseguir la gloria eterna en el culto de cualquier religión . . ." [97] The kindly but intolerant bishop then cites a series of encyclicals and allocutions in which this proposition is condemned.

I hope that it is now evident that the religious opinions expressed in *Gloria* show a constant and close resemblance to *krausista* religious principles. This impression could be reinforced by an examination of *krausismo* in Galdós' other novels. In *La familia de León Roch* we have a hero who tries to regulate his life on the *krausista* code of ethics, one which is based on reason and philosophy, not religion, and who wishes to dedicate his life to humanity. In a later novel (*El doctor Centeno*) Galdós drew a picture of a *krausista* educator, Jesús Delgado. Although he is mad, his ideas on education are perfectly sound, suffering only from the fact that they are a hundred years ahead of their times. The *krausista* ideal of the lay saint, to which León Roch aspires, shows itself as at least a partial influence in the character of Orozco (*La incógnita* and *Realidad*).[98]

[96] *Ibid.*, p. 638 (II, 20).

[97] *Ibid.*, p. 560 (I, 30).

[98] José Yxart, *El arte escénico en España*, Barcelona, 1894, p. 316. Here Orozco is described as a "variante del 'santo krausista' que tiene su homogéneo en *Locura o santidad* y su filiación en algunas otras novelas de Pérez Galdós, influidas sucesivamente por sistemas filosóficos coetáneos . . ." *Cf.* M. de la Revilla, "Los santos de la humanidad," in *El Correo de España*, Mar. 28, 1871. He calls men like Socrates, Washington, Galileo, Watt, and

But it might be asked if these ideas are the unique property of *krausismo*; in other words, could it be possible that Galdós got them not from *krausismo* but from other philosophies which preached the same religious concepts. There are many other philosophic currents which reinforce the fundamental concepts of *krausismo*, but this latter creed remains the central, unifying core of Galdós' religious beliefs. To illustrate this point I shall have to summarize the philosophic currents of the period in Spain.

Up to the advent of *krausismo* (*c.* 1850) nineteenth-century Spain had been practically an ideological wasteland. The one notable exception, the Catholic apologist and precursor of Thomism, Jaime Balmes, himself complained that philosophic studies had been long abandoned in Spain.[99] Next we have a period of about twenty years (1850–1870) dominated by *krausismo*. There are of course a few minor currents – the Hegelians Castelar and Pi y Margall, a few eclectic philosophers, and a few Catalan positivists. But the very tolerance of the "orthodox" *krausista* school caused its rapid breakup. Its attitude was that all philosophies should be encouraged, that they all contained some truth. Hence about 1870–1880 many followers of Sanz del Río set out in new directions. The influential critic Manuel de la Revilla became a neo-Kantian; positivistic systems based on Comte, Darwin, and Spencer had their followers; even those who still called themselves *krausistas* admitted many new ideas from diverse sources.

The awakened interest in science, popularized especially through the works of Darwin and Flammarion, brought many repercussions into Spain. Thomism or scholasticism began to flourish again. *Krausismo* continued to exist (in fact, it still exists in

Voltaire saints. Although the church asks us to hate some of these men, humanity should honor them in the inner temple of the conscience, the seat of "la eterna religión que a nadie excomulga ni condena."

As an epigraph he cites Salmerón: "No solamente hay santos en la religión: los hay también en las demás esferas de la vida: hay santos en el arte; hay santos en la moral; hay santos en la ciencia; hay santos en la política; porque santo es todo aquel que consagra su vida y su pensamiento al cumplimiento del bien, sólo por puro motivo del bien mismo."

[99] *Cartas a un escéptico* . . ., p. 141.

Spain) diffused by the *Institución libre de enseñanza* and similar educational centers, but it was considerably modified and mixed with new currents of thought. By 1881 a writer who describes the philosophical currents of contemporary Spain states that there are but two main ones: the officially accepted current of Thomism and the unorthodox stream of positivism. The latter was especially appealing to young men in its English form as represented by Herbert Spencer. Notice that *krausismo* is no longer named as a principal philosophic trend.[100]

What I have been saying on the history of philosophy in Spain is well put by Clarín: "La filosofía en España era en rigor planta exótica; puede decirse que la trajo consigo de Alemania el ilustre Sanz del Río . . . La filosofía del siglo, la única que podía ser algo más que una momia, un ser vivo, entró en España con la influencia de las escuelas idealistas importada por el filósofo citado. Cuando ya por el mundo corrían con más crédito que los sistemas de los grandes filósofos idealistas de Alemania las derivaciones de la izquierda hegeliana y el positivismo francés y el inglés, en España la escuela krausista prosperaba, y con riguroso método, gran pureza de miras y parsimoniosa investigación, iba propagando un espíritu filosófico, de cuya fecundidad en buenas obras y buenos pensamientos no pueden tener exacta idea los contemporáneos, ni aun los que más de cerca y más imparcialmente estudien este influjo, insensible para los observadores poco atentos. Como oposición necesaria del krausismo, que sin ella podría degenerar en dogmatismo de secta intolerante, llegaron después las corrientes de otros sistemas, tales como el monismo, el spencerismo, el darwinismo, etc., etc., y hoy tenemos ya, por fortuna, muestra de todas las escuelas . . ." [101]

Let us take a clear example of a philosophical trend which reinforced an idea already present in *krausismo*. Galdós possessed Camille Flammarion's *La pluralité des mondes habités* in the edition of 1865. That he read the book is obvious: he mentions it twice by name in *Fortunata y Jacinta* and names Flammarion

[100] E. Sanz y Escartín, in *Revista de España*, 83 (1881), 392–410.
[101] *Solos de Clarín*, p. 70.

with an allusion to this book in *Doña Perfecta.* Now the French astronomer is a believer in God, but as in the case of the *krausistas,* his God exists "indépendamment de tout dogme, nous dirions même indépendamment de toute idée religieuse . . ."[102] He often objects to dogma and metaphysics and declares that the schools and sects which oppose his doctrine will be dispersed by scientific enlightenment.[103] Astronomy holds the keys to the domain of religion and has laid the foundations of the philosophy of the future.[104] Here we recall the *krausistas*' insistence on a *future* universal creed and Daniel Morton's desperate last search for the religion of the future.

God is Spirit, as Jesus said to the Samaritan woman. This, according to Flammarion (and Renan before him) is the foundation of the religion of humanity which will be the religion of the inhabitants of other planets. Almost the same idea occurs in Sanz del Río's adaptation of Krause's fundamental work, *Ideal de la humanidad para la vida*: "Dios quiere, y la razón y la naturaleza lo muestran, que sobre cada cuerpo planetario, en que la naturaleza ha engendrado su más perfecta criatura, el cuerpo humano, el espíritu se reuna en sus individuos a la naturaleza, en *unión esencial, en humanidad* . . ." The humanity of each planet is part of universal humanity, sharing the same ideals. Ultimately all humanity will be united in a single universal human cult.[105]

Another French thinker whose works enjoyed a great popularity during Galdós' youth was Renan. At the time of the publi-

[102] Flammarion, *La pluralité des mondes habités,* p. 131.

[103] *Ibid.,* pp. 336 and 349.

[104] *Ibid.,* p. 319.

[105] Sanz del Río, *Ideal de la humanidad para la vida,* p. 35. The same ideas formed the basis of the spiritualist cult, which had thousands of adherents at this time in Spain, and counted influential army officers, *diputados,* and literary men in its numbers (see M. Pelayo, *Heterodoxos,* ed. Artigas, VII, 497). The spiritualists thought that the inhabitants of other planets were the transmigrated souls of people who had lived here on the earth. They denied the existence of the devil and of hell (on which point Galdós and the *krausistas* agreed with them; see Berkowitz, *Pérez Galdós,* p. 73) and looked forward to the establishments of "la Iglesia universal de Jesús" (see M. Pelayo, pp. 490 and 496). Works of the spiritualists appeared prominently in magazines of the times. (See, for example, "La religión laica" in the *Revista Europea,* 1878. This work, although after *Gloria,* shows what

cation of his *Vie de Jésus* a whole series of Spanish critiques – mostly refutations – appeared.[106] About the time *Gloria* was being written, Renan's name was again appearing frequently in Spanish periodicals, first because of the dispute over his unsuccessful campaign for election to the French Academy, and then because of the publication of the various volumes of his *Origines du Christianisme*. As a constant reader in the Ateneo, Galdós could hardly have overlooked Renan, and once knowing him would have inevitably been led to the *Vie de Jésus*. However, a copy of this work does not exist today in Galdós' private library.

Renan's religious views show a striking and constant parallelism to those we have seen in *Gloria*. He declares that the proper interpretation of Jesus' teaching is "un culte pur, une religion sans prêtres et sans pratiques extérieures, reposant toute sur les sentiments du coeur, sur l'imitation de Dieu, sur le rapport immédiat de la conscience avec le Père celeste . . . Jamais on n'a été moins prêtre que ne le fut Jésus, jamais ennemi des formes qui étouffent la religion sous prétexte de la protéger . . . Une idée absolument neuve, l'idée d'un culte fondé sur la pureté du coeur et sur la fraternité humaine, faisait par lui son entrée dans le monde; idée tellement élevée, que l'Église chrétienne devait sur ce point trahir complètement les intentions de son chef . . ."[107] This religion was not for one race or tribe but for all mankind: "La religion de l'humanité, établie non sur le sang, mais sur le coeur, est fondée."[108]

When Jesus explained to the woman of Sichem that the time

the spiritualists were preaching. It advocates a religion without creed, bigger and more embracing than any then known with the possible exception of Unitarianism. It is by the Vizconde de Torres Solanot, the leader of the Madrid spiritualist group.) Thus undoubtedly Galdós knew and was sympathetic to some of the spiritualists' thought.

Flammarion's doctrines provoked a retort by the Canon N. Alonso Perujo, *La pluralidad de los mundos habitados ante la fe católica*, Madrid, 1877.

[106] Luis Vidart, *La filosofía española – Indicaciones bibliográficas*, Madrid, 1866, Part II, section called "Refutaciones de las doctrinas filosóficas de Mr. Renan"; see also Pereda's youthful article against the *Vie de Jésus*, which was then running serially in a Spanish newspaper, published in Pereda, *Obras completas*, ed. Aguilar, pp. 103–105.

[107] Renan, *Vie de Jésus*, n.d., p. 89.

[108] *Ibid.*, p. 232.

had come when men would worship neither on the mountain (as did the Samaritans) nor in Jerusalem (as the Jews) but in their hearts and spirits, he reached the apex of his sublime mission. "Il dit pour la première fois le mot sur lequel reposera l'édifice de la religion éternelle. Il fonda le culte . . . que pratiqueront toutes les ames élevées jusqu'à la fin des temps. Non-seulement sa religion ce jour-là, fut la bonne religion de l'humanité, ce fut la religion absolue . . ." [109] This is the religion which will prevail in heaven.[110] He turned his back on dogmatic and intolerant Judaism [111] to give the new commandment of his new religion: "Love ye one another as I have loved you." [112]

Renan's creed has in common with Galdós' the insistence on the spirit of religion, the importance of the conscience, the harmfulness of dogma or man-made rules, and the ultimate establishment on earth of this perfect religion which already exists in heaven and which sees the brotherhood of all humanity as its highest practical objective. In these points Renan's thought also parallels *krausismo*.

Another philosopher who believed that Christianity must give way to a new faith was Edward von Hartmann. His *Religion of the Future* (1874) was soon widely known in both the original and translations. In Spanish garb it first appeared in the *Revista Europea*, from January to March 1877, that is, in time to have influenced the second part of *Gloria* (written in March, April, and May 1877) in whose last pages Galdós advocates a single universal religion, the religion of the future.

Hartmann argues that a new faith, not a reconstruction of old Christianity, is necessary. Catholicism is out of touch with modern civilization (science) and therefore is a lifeless mummy. Liberal Protestantism is neither Christian nor religious, although it is a transitional step toward the future religion as it establishes an ethical code independent of metaphysics. What is needed is a new universal faith based on pantheism and combining the best

[109] *Ibid.*, p. 243.
[110] *Ibid.*, p. 296.
[111] *Ibid.*, p. 426
[112] *Ibid.*, p. 402.

of Oriental religion (Brahmanism) with the best of the Judeo-Christian tradition. Its God would be impersonal, immanent in all the universe; its moral code would be based on doing good to everyone, including oneself, derived from self-interest, and founded on the oneness of the God-pervaded universe.[113]

Obviously Galdós is not writing a treatise on philosophy in *Gloria.* Starting from an outraged feeling of the injustice of the present system, nourished by his contacts with *krausismo* and his readings of Flammarion and Renan, he attacks intolerance on an emotional basis in the first part of his novel. Then came the labored second part, where, especially in the closing pages, he tries consciously to underline the philosophical theme of his book. But perfection lies far off in the misty future. To seek a solution of the religious problem here and now is madness: witness the strange malady from which Daniel dies, seeking "una religión nueva, la religión única, la religión del porvenir."[114] This religion does exist in heaven and we should aspire to make it exist as much as possible on earth.

Here, if anywhere, are reminiscences of Hartmann, along with a criticism of the visionary nature of his system. The German philosopher calls for an amalgamation of religions. Galdós produces a practical fusion of two religions in Jesús, the child of Daniel and Gloria, who, like Juanita Lund, is "la personificación más hermosa de la humanidad emancipada de los antagonismos

[113] That Hartmann interested the Spaniards is evident from the number of times they cite him. His name appears frequently in José del Perojo's *Ensayos sobre el movimiento intelectual en Alemania*, Madrid, 1875. He is named by M. Pelayo in *La Tertulia*, I (1877), 159. Articles by Hartmann appear in the *Revista Europea*, VII (1876), pp. 7 and 65; and in the *Revista Contemporánea*, I (1875), and VII (Jan.–Feb. 1877). Finally, an exposition of his system is published in the last-named magazine, II (Feb.–Mar. 1876). His *Religion of the Future* was twice translated in 1877 – by A. Zozaya in the series *Biblioteca Económica Filosófica*, tomo 39; and by Armando Palacio Valdés (see *Illustración Española y Americana*, XXI [Apr. 15, 1877], 254). Since Palacio Valdés was then a constant contributor to the *Revista Europea*, we may assume that the translation anonymously published there is his work, later issued in book form.

Galdós knew something about Hartmann before writing *Gloria*: witness the inclusion of his name as an example of a modern philosopher in *Doña Perfecta*, Chap. 9 (*Obras completas*, Aguilar, IV, 26).

[114] *Gloria*, p. 678 (II, 33).

religiosos por virtud del amor."[115] But these general resemblances are not sufficient for us to state categorically that Galdós felt the influence of Hartmann's *Religion of the Future*. If he knew the work, and to me it seems probable that he did, its ideas served to confirm and strengthen thoughts already present in his mind.

The ideas of Flammarion, Renan, and Hartmann may not be the only currents of thought which served to strengthen the principles of *krausismo*.[116] Galdós probably knew the thought of all these men; he could hardly open a magazine without finding some article on or by one of them. But he would be especially aware of them because of the Ateneo discussions.

On November 30, 1876, in the *Sección de ciencias morales y políticas*, which was then under the presidency of the well-known *krausista* Gumersindo de Azcárate, the debate turned from the appointed subject, namely the government of England, to the importance of religious reform in that country. Figuerola maintained that Protestantism brought new ideas into government, without which "quizá viviría todavía Europa en la especie de nihilismo político y religioso en que yacía."[117] He went on to praise the reformers for putting the emphasis on practical morality and not devoting their time to the explanation of the dogmas, as do the Catholics. These ideas and other similar ones were

[115] *Ibid.*, p. 679 (II, 33).

[116] In Galdós' library was F. Laurent, *Études sur l'histoire de l'humanité*, 1861–1870, which was probably one of the youthful Spaniard's source books for current philosophical knowledge. (See above p. 12.) Volume XVII of the work, entitled "La religion de l'avenir," summarizes all the philosophies prior to its publication, devoting much space to Renan, Strauss, Channing, and many others whose ideas had many points of contact with *krausismo*. Hartmann, of course, wrote after Laurent, but the two men's works are very similar in organization and ideas.

Galdós may possibly have noted the following passage in Laurent's work (Vol. I, "L'Orient," p. 374, in the section titled *Les Hébreux*): "Le christianisme est la religion de l'autre monde. De son côté, le mosaïsme est trop exclusivement une religion de ce monde. Ce sera à la religion de l'avenir à concilier les deux éléments qui constituent la vie." Here we have suggested the religious problem of *Gloria*. We shall see later that Galdós read widely on the Jews before undertaking his novel; hence it is probable that he reread this section of a book he already knew and had at hand on his bookshelf.

[117] See *Boletín del Ateneo. Organo oficial del Ateneo de Madrid*, I, 48.

warmly combated by Padre Miguel Sánchez and defended by Figuerola on December 7.[118] The debate continued throughout the month. This was the sort of thing that Galdós heard constantly not only in the formal meetings of the Ateneo, but in endless corridor conversations.[119]

Now when the plan of *Gloria* flashed into Galdós' mind he was walking between the Calle de la Montera (where the Ateneo was then situated) and the Café Universal. Had he come from the Ateneo? Had a discussion on modern philosophical trends and the religious problem started his mind working on his half-planned novel? We shall never know the exact facts of the case, but we are probably justified in saying that he came symbolically from the Ateneo if not in reality. From its library, its debates, and its informal discussion he brought a knowledge of modern philosophy which is the foundation on which *Gloria* is built.

KRAUSISMO IN OTHER NOVELS

Gloria appeared not long after notable events had taken place in Spain. The Bourbons were restored in the person of Alfonso XII (1875); the second Carlist war was brought to an end; the triumphant dynasty revoked the complete liberty in religion which was inaugurated by the Revolution of 1868. Then, under the instigation of the neo-Catholic press, the government removed many of the *krausista* professors from their university chairs.

This action was almost a death blow to the "orthodox" *krausista* group, but its members found many new spheres of activity in which they strove to propagate the philosophical spirit. Some

[118] *Ibid.*, I, 78–79.

[119] See Galdós' description of the Ateneo in *Prim,* Chaps. 12 and 13. In the Ateneo season after the publication of *Gloria* the debate was even more pertinent to our theme. The subject of discussion was "¿Estará destinada a desaparecer de los dominios de la razón y la conciencia la religión cristiana? Si debe desaparecer, ¿qué religión será la que ocupe su lugar? ¿O es que habrá de realizarse un renacimiento religioso cristiano?" See *Boletín del Ateneo,* I, 587; and *El Parlamento,* issue of Nov. 9, 1877, article called "El Ateneo." Of course this discussion could not contribute to *Gloria,* but since it is the climax of a long series of earlier arguments, it shows the direction of intellectual currents even before its date.

turned to politics, but those who interest us remained in the more intellectual fields of education and literature. The saintly Francisco Giner de los Ríos founded, with a group of the dismissed professors, the *Institución libre de enseñanza* (1876), surely *krausismo*'s most valuable and noble contribution to Spain. The Ateneo debates on philosophy and religion became an outlet for the teachers who had no classroom.[120] In 1876 they reached a high pitch of intensity and interest. Finally, the novel became a medium by which the *krausistas* sought to carry their message to the people. In their general disillusionment, the liberals realized that they must draw back their lines and begin a long campaign of propaganda and education to prepare for the next advance.

It is in the light of these events that we must interpret two attempts to portray sympathetically the *krausista* freethinker in religious novels which appeared just before *Gloria*. These were *La novela de Luis* (1876) by S. de Villarminio and the *Minuta de un testamento*, publicada y anotada por W . . . (1876). The latter was the work of Gumersindo de Azcárate, one of the "separated" professors and an important collaborator in the new *Institución libre de enseñanza*, whom we have just met in the Ateneo. Menéndez Pelayo quickly saw the resemblance between these novels and *Gloria*. He states that Galdós has become an imitator, not as usual of Balzac or Dickens, but of Villarminio, "autor de la *Novela de Luis*, que es, de todas las novelas que conozco, la más próxima a *Gloria* . . ." and exclaims, "¡Oh y cuán triste cosa es no ver más mundo que el que se ve desde el ahumado recinto del Ateneo, y ponerse a hacer novelas de carácter y costumbres con personajes de la *Minuta de un testamento*, como si Ficóbriga fuese un país de Salmerones o de Azcárates!"[121] An examination of the two novels will, I believe, convince us that their *ambiente moral* and philosophy are identical to those of *Gloria*, but there are certainly no direct borrowings of characters, plot situations, or language.

[120] See V. García Martí, *El Ateneo de Madrid*, pp. 144–147; also R. M. de Labra, "El Ateneo de Madrid," in *Revista Contemporánea*, XV (1878), esp. 347–351.

[121] Menéndez Pelayo, *Heterodoxos*, ed. Artigas, VII, 486–487.

La novela de Luis[122] tells the story of a man, left an orphan at sixteen, who was sent to Germany to study and then to serve an apprenticeship in a great business. The simplicity and honesty of German customs and the love of work, music, and nature all influence profoundly the formation of Luis' character. He passes through England on his way home and is enthusiastic in his praise of English business activity and home life. Once back in his native city, Málaga(?), he avoids marriage with Dolores, the fanatically religious daughter of his guardian. He soon discovers that Spanish society is cruel to anyone who thinks for himself, that religion is above all the observance of dogma, and that many rituals are in poor artistic taste.[123]

Luis was not an atheist, but his profound and sincere religion was quite different from Spanish Catholicism. He believed in a life of dedication to the ideal, "no en la práctica de determinadas exterioridades religiosas, ni en la creencia de determinados dogmas, que nada tienen que ver con la conducta del hombre."[124] The neo-Catholics soon undermine Luis' credit at home and abroad, so that the bank refuses to honor his signature. Luis marries Lucila Waldemar, daughter of a German family living in Spain, and retires with his wife and children to the one property he still possesses in the village of Benaláh. Here he devotes himself to the improvement of agriculture, popular education, and propaganda toward freedom of worship and of teaching. Largely through his efforts the backward village becomes a garden spot. All the villagers mourn sincerely Luis' death.

Azcárate's work, *Minuta de un testamento*, is, in construction, even poorer than *La novela de Luis*. The author says he has found and will publish with annotations a will of unusual form. It consists of three parts, the first (and by far the most important)

[122] Menéndez Pelayo (*Heterodoxos*, VII, 465, n. 1) says that the name "Villarminio" seems to be a pseudonym, and adds, "Lo que nadie podrá disputar al Sr. de Villarminio es el haber precedido al autor de *Gloria* y *La familia de León Roch*, en atacar insidiosamente al catolicismo por medio de novelas." He also calls *La novela de Luis* "hermana gemela de la *Minuta de un testamento*."

[123] S. de Villarminio, *La novela de Luis*, Madrid, 1876, pp. 91, 102–103, and 107.

[124] *Ibid.*, p. 131.

being the life of the testator, the second, the disposition of his properties, and the third, his last advice to his children. Within the first part, the initial chapter, dealing with the religious life of the deceased, is much the longest and most significant. The testator was a doctor of medicine and professor of physiology in a provincial Spanish university. From earliest youth he had doubts about religion but never ceased believing in God and admiring Christianity. He marries an orthodox Catholic and has three children. His hope that he can return to orthodoxy comes to naught; he then reveals his religious beliefs to his wife, showing her at the same time how it is possible for him, a freethinker, to live in peace and harmony with a Catholic believer.

This message of tolerance is really the essence of the whole book. Dogmatic religion and superstitious performance of ritual are constantly decried, while loving one's fellowmen and living according to Christian principles are extolled.[125] Azcárate shows a strong leaning toward Unitarianism which blends very well with his *krausismo*.

What relationship, if any, is there between *Gloria* and the works of Villarminio and Azcárate? I believe it is mostly the tenuous resemblance between works produced by authors of the same viewpoint in the same historical circumstances. The two novels we have just examined show that there was an urgent desire to put the religious problem before the people in artistic form. Freedom of worship had failed in Spain. The particular classes which most impeded progress were the aristocracy and enriched bourgeoisie, the groups which held strongly to neo-Catholic traditionalism. Their influence must be combated and the Spanish people must be prepared for progress.

In my mind there is no doubt that *La novela de Luis* and the *Minuta de un testamento* mark stages in this campaign.[126] But to say that *Gloria* is just another propaganda novel is to go too far. The didactic purpose is obvious, but there is a great difference in

[125] Azcárate, *Minuta de un testamento*, pp. 52–53 and 128.

[126] Another novel showing the same philosophic trend is U. González Serrano's translation of Auerbach's *Benito Espinosa*, also published just before *Gloria*. We shall examine it in detail later on.

the way Galdós presents his propaganda to us. He hopes for a perfect religion in the distant future, but not until many Glorias have succumbed as victims to fanaticism and intolerance. In other words, Galdós has his feet upon the earth and sees all the practical difficulties in the way of religious reform. He sees how the germ of intolerance, even in gentle folk, can wax into a demon of violence.

There is a marked contrast between the realism of Galdós' handling of the propaganda theme and the idealism of the other two novels. Both Luis and the will-maker solve the problem of intolerance in their own families and to a considerable extent with their neighbors. For example, Luis, although he is persecuted by the neo-Catholic upper classes in his home city, wins the love of all his fellow citizens in the village of Benaláh. But, above all, the peaceful resolution of the religious problem with the orthodox wife in the *Minuta de un testamento* is hard to accept. It *could* be possible, as in the Lund family, but in traditionalistic Spain, it would not be likely.

Galdós in *Gloria* and later in *La familia de León Roch* gives us his realistic version of what would happen if a conflict of religious ideas came between lovers or spouses. In each case he shows us that the solution depends not alone on the interested parties, but also on their families, friends, and the *ambiente moral.* That Galdós was aware of the practical difficulties of the religious problem is evident in the following statement on the subject matter of literature which he made in 1870, on the eve of his career as a novelist: "Descuella en primer lugar el problema religioso, que perturba los hogares y ofrece contradicciones que asustan; porque mientras en una parte la falta de creencias afloja o rompe los lazos morales y civiles que forman la familia, en otras produce los mismos efectos el fanatismo y las costumbres devotas." [127]

To sum up, Galdós had two predecessors in the field of the *krausista* novel. Both of these works failed because they lost contact with the reality of life and because they were poorly organ-

[127] *Revista de España,* XV (1870), 167.

ized and abounded in long philosophical discourses. Galdós, much more the novelist than the philosopher, avoids these pitfalls. The human reaction, seen within the surrounding *ambiente moral*, is his chief interest and he holds his expressions of philosophy down to the minimum consistent with his characters and theme. In a sense his *Gloria* is a continuation of the propagandistic trend of Villarminio and Azcárate, but at the same time it is an artistic reaction against them.

SHIPWRECKS

It is now time to return to the harbor of Ficóbriga for the shipwreck of the steamer *Plantagenet* and to notice the change which Galdós introduces into his concept of the harbor during the course of his narrative. To me, this alteration is one of the seams or joints in Don Benito's raw material, one which he failed to weld skillfully enough to make it invisible.

In the original description a winding estuary empties into the poorly protected bay beside the peninsula of Ficóbriga. This *ría* is navigable, although with difficulty. "Escaso número de buques navega en sus pobres aguas, y sabe Dios el trabajo que les cuesta dar dos pasos dentro de aquella angosta callejuela, cuando se duerme el viento y la corriente empuja hacia la peligrosa barra."[128] Although the boats in this description are sailing craft, steamers also enter the *ría*, as sometimes from her home Gloria hears "el silbato lejano de un vapor zarpando de la ría . . ."[129] Yet when the *Plantagenet* (whose small size may be judged from her complement of seven officers and men) appears off Ficóbriga seeking shelter from the storm, one of the fishermen explains that "El *Plantagenet* no puede entrar en esta ría . . . quiso guarecerse en el abra de Ficóbriga . . ."[130] But as the ship approaches the roadway it loses its rudder and is crushed against the line of rocks (los Camellos) at the end of the peninsula.

This seemingly trivial oversight really marks the entrance of a

[128] *Gloria*, p. 499 (I, 1).
[129] *Ibid.*, p. 517 (I, 12).
[130] *Ibid.*, p. 527 (I, 17).

new element into the complex of materials from which Galdós constructed *Gloria.* Among the books in his private library was Octave Feuillet's *Histoire de Sibylle* in the edition of 1874, and there is evidence (a paper place marker, some pencil lines) that the book was read. In one of the early reviews of *Gloria,* Manuel de la Revilla points out that Galdós and Feuillet deal with the same problem and come to the same solution.[131] Although he gives credit to Feuillet for priority, he believes that Galdós' treatment of the theme is far more powerful. Nowhere does he suggest that Galdós actually incorporated suggestions from Feuillet's work into *Gloria,* which is what I now intend to prove.

The French novel is, in brief, the account of a love affair between a stoutly Catholic girl (Sibylle) and a freethinker (Raoul). It is written from a sentimentally Catholic point of view, reflecting the tolerant, unexaggerated French attitude which contrasts strongly with the *neocatolicismo* of Spain. Feuillet does not see any reason why his Catholic heroine should not be taught by a Protestant tutor,[132] does not deny non-Catholics admittance into heaven,[133] and does not see any religious obstacle to a marriage between a believer and a nonbeliever.[134] It is then on grounds of sentiment – attachment to family tradition, love of ritual, fear of abandonment by a husband not restrained by religion[135] – that Sibylle refuses to marry Raoul. As she wastes slowly away under the emotional strain of this situation she conceives the notion that her death will bring Raoul into the fold. This in fact is the dénoûment of the novel.

There is a shipwreck in the *Histoire de Sibylle* which has surprising analogies to that of *Gloria.* The heroine of the French novel lives on the Norman coast near the village of Férias. Here there is a small church, surrounded by a graveyard, near the edge of a cliff overlooking the small harbor. This harbor con-

[131] *Revista Contemporánea,* IX (1877), 379.
[132] *Histoire de Sibylle* (Oeuvres complètes d'Octave Feuillet de l'Academie Française), Paris, Calmann-Lévy, n.d., p. 50.
[133] *Ibid.,* p. 84.
[134] *Ibid.,* p. 327.
[135] *Ibid.,* pp. 276 and 327.

sists of an inner basin, which is protected by jetties and capable of receiving only the smallest of fishing smacks, and the outer harbor, which is insecure and unsheltered, but which offers ". . . une certaine sécurité relative, grâce à une série de roches et de hauts-fonds qui la fermaient d'un côte, et lui formaient, en s'avançant au loin dans la mer, une sorte de jetée naturelle."[136]

One stormy Sunday evening when most of the villagers are just coming out of vesper services in the church they see a large fishing boat, already badly damaged by the gale, which tries to double the point of rocks and ride out the storm in the relative calm of the roadway. Unfortunately it is wrecked on these very rocks.

Sibylle's grandfather, a respected country nobleman, fails to stimulate the fishermen to undertake a rescue, even when he offers liberal rewards.[137] The village priest also is unsuccessful at first and must content himself with giving absolution to, and praying for, the unknown crew of the bark. But he then leads his flock down to the beach and, when the sailors still hesitate to risk their lives, he insists on going himself to the rescue. One old salt, who had seemed absolutely indifferent to the fate of the shipwrecked mariners up to this point, joins the curé, and then everyone wants to go too. A crew is chosen, rows out to the wreck, and effects the rescue. The bystanders are highly edified by the noble bearing of the priest.[138]

To tell the story of the shipwreck in *Gloria* is to repeat much of the story just told, although there are inevitable differences. A group sets out from the church of Ficóbriga to walk on the beach. They depart before the storm breaks but are forced to seek shelter in the hut of the customs guard. From this point they witness the approach of the *Plantagenet* which tries to find shelter behind *Los Camellos*. In the group are two priests, the saintly old bishop, Don Angel, who prays for the mariners, and the robust Don Silvestre Romero, who leads the rescue. Among the sailors and fishermen who gather on the beach to watch

[136] *Ibid.*, p. 92.
[137] *Ibid.*, p. 93.
[138] *Ibid.*, pp. 92–99 (Chap. 7).

the misfortune of the *Plantagenet* is one old salt who acts as the spokesman for the seafarers and refuses to undertake the rescue. After the priest volunteers all are eager to accompany him. As in *Sibylle*, the emotional effect of the rescue is highly edifying.[139]

It scarcely need be said that shipwrecks all have some elements in common—the immense waves, the lashing wind, the leaden sky, etc.[140] But in *Gloria* and *Sibylle* we have two exceptional elements which would not be apt to appear merely by chance. They are the topographical factor and the rescue by the priest. It is true that many a shipwreck takes place within sight of the port, especially in literature. But the exact situation—the wrecking of the ship on rocks behind which it could find shelter—is not so common.

And here we must consider again the alteration of the Ficobrigan harbor. If the ship could have run into the *ría*, as was possible at the beginning of our tale, it could have swung wide of *Los Camellos*. Perhaps it would still have been wrecked—after all its rudder was now useless—but it would have been a different wreck on the beach or the sand bar at the mouth of the *ría*. The rescue would then have been completely different, and might have been accomplished even without the use of a boat. But when Galdós makes it impossible for the *Plantagenet* to enter the *ría*, he forces it to try for shelter behind the rocks and makes the wreck and the rescue both follow the pattern of Feuillet's novel. Had Galdós worked more slowly, he doubtless would have deleted from the early chapters of his book the two phrases which speak of navigation of the *ría*. Had this been done I do not believe we should ever have been able to prove

[139] *Gloria*, Pt. I, Chaps. 17 and 18.

[140] Effie L. Erickson ("The Influence of Charles Dickens on Galdós," *Hispania*, XIX [1939], 421–430) sees a close parallel between the shipwreck in *David Copperfield* (Chap. 55) and the one in *Gloria*. On page 429 she says: "There are scenes like that of the shipwreck in *Gloria* . . . which seem to show not only influence but direct 'borrowing'." But in Dickens' work the ship is wrecked on a beach, far from the harbor. Although an attempt is made to swim a line out to the boat, no rescue is effected. All those on the ship are drowned. Finally, Dickens devotes much more attention to the description of the storm as a phenomenon of nature than Galdós does.

that Galdós had the *Histoire de Sibylle* in his mind as one of the elements which crystallized into the pattern of *Gloria.* We might have suspected it then, but now I think we can take it for granted.

PRIESTS–FRENCH AND SPANISH

The only part of *Gloria* which parallels step by step the action of *Sibylle* is the shipwreck scene. But once we admit on this basis that there is a relationship between the two novels it is apparent that three of Galdós' characters have notable similarities to those of Feuillet. Gloria resembles Sibylle, as we shall see later on; and the two priests, D. Angel and D. Silvestre, resemble l'abbé Renaud. The two Spanish priests, however, are a *dédoublement* of the Frenchman's character, in that his best qualities are given to D. Angel while his weaknesses all go to D. Silvestre. Of this division we already had a hint in the rescue scene, where D. Angel prays and blesses while D. Silvestre does the physical part of the rescue. In the French work l'abbé Renaud acts both of these roles.

The French priest was at the time of Sibylle's birth an "homme robuste, déjà mûr et dont let visage respirait une honnête bonhomie . . ."[141] He was of peasant stock; hence he found in his friendly relations with the country nobility a satisfaction which at first precluded further spiritual development.[142] Furthermore, he was above all a *bon vivant*, enjoying to the utmost his invitations to dinner, his coffee, his game of billiards or whist.[143] His theology is so weak that when Sibylle asks questions about religious mysteries, he has to go back to his books to refresh his memory.[144] Sibylle is in fact shocked by the innocent worldliness of the curé and does not realize the fundamental nobility of his nature until she sees him lead the rescue. Soon afterwards she confesses to him the impression which he had formerly made on her, and as a result the abbé gives up all of his dearest

[141] *Histoire de Sibylle*, p. 2.
[142] *Ibid.*, p. 111.
[143] *Ibid.*, p. 109.
[144] *Ibid.*, p. 73

pleasures. He refuses invitations to dinner;[145] abjures his coffee;[146] becomes solemn[147] and thin.[148] His constant reading of the church fathers gives a new life to his discussions of creed.[149] He has also aged considerably and gives the over-all impression of a frail, childlike, saintly old man.[150]

Owing to the "conversion" of the abbé Renaud we really have two separate character phases in him – the robust *bon vivant* and the sweet, childlike saint. This is the division which Galdós made. To D. Silvestre Romero he attributed the first element, although he did not hesitate to embroider the theme with numerous additions. Romero was robust, young, filled with animal spirits.[151] He lived most comfortably and interested himself particularly in food, the symbol of his plenty being his well-stocked country residence, el Soto de Briján, where all the fruits and domestic animals of the region flourished.[152] This possession is the scene of the stupendous banquet which D. Silvestre offers the gentry of Ficóbriga.[153]

D. Silvestre was born into a peasant family in the wild mountainous region of the Picos de Europa.[154] Galdós himself had visited the region only a few months before undertaking Gloria.[155] He mentions, in passing, the bears which inhabit the area; he could also have mentioned the *rebecos* (mountain goats), the salmon, and many other animals and fish which make the region a sportsman's paradise.

I shall establish later why Galdós gave D. Silvestre this origin. Having given him such an origin, Galdós quite logically makes him a vigorous man. As a boy hunting and fishing were his life; now he still makes them his chief diversion. Note that this trait

[145] *Ibid.*, p. 114.
[146] *Ibid.*, p. 115.
[147] *Ibid.*, p. 116.
[148] *Ibid.*, p. 119.
[149] *Ibid.*, p. 121.
[150] *Ibid.*, pp. 120–125.
[151] *Gloria*, p. 528 (I, 18).
[152] *Ibid.*, pp. 528 and 530 (I, 18).
[153] *Ibid.*, p. 565 (I, 33).
[154] *Ibid.*, p. 529 (I, 18).
[155] *Cuarenta leguas*, in *Obras completas*, Aguilar, VI, 1506.

harmonizes well with his love of good and varied food. His other interest is politics; like many a Spanish priest he is the local *cacique*.[156] He, too, is weak in theology and cannot prove his points without recourse to his books.[157] The people of the town like him because he dispatches his mass quickly and because, although not a saint, he is a gentleman.[158]

The saintly qualities of the abbé Renaud reappear in D. Angel de Lantigua. Galdó starts his description of him with "El obispo parecía un niño grande" and throughout he stresses the *bonhomie*, the naïve sweetness, of the man.[159] He is so kindly he can hardly realize that some people are bad. He loves books of piety but hates newspapers. He never takes an active part in politics. His taste and intelligence are not of the highest, but he has a great love of his fellowmen which redeems all.[160]

We should now notice a certain artistic incongruity in Galdós' conception of Silvestre Romero. His rescue of the shipwrecked mariners is indeed a courageous act, but it is the isolated good deed of a man who is not particularly admirable before and who becomes even despicable afterwards. Had the rescue been presented to us as a feat of animal courage it would have been in keeping with the over-all artistic conception of D. Silvestre. Instead of this, we find that the principal witnesses of the act are filled with the keenest and purest Christian sentiments, which is apparently the emotion Galdós wants us as readers to experience. Yet D. Silvestre soon begins to boast of his part in the rescue and even sends anonymous letters to the newspapers describing it.[161] His unscrupulous political activity and *gourmandise* increase. Hence there is an artistic deception about the edification the author made us feel at the time of the rescue.[162] Such is not the case in the French novel, as the rescue is the beginning of the sanctification of the curé. In short, we are forced

[156] *Gloria*, p. 529 (I, 18).
[157] *Ibid.*, p. 537 (I, 21).
[158] *Ibid.*, pp. 528–529 (I, 18).
[159] *Ibid.*, p. 513 (I, 10).
[160] *Ibid.*, p. 514 (I, 10).
[161] *Ibid.*, p. 540 (I, 22).
[162] *Ibid.*, p. 530 (I, 18).

to conclude that Galdós falsified the character of D. Silvestre by following the French novel too closely.

I should not like to give the impression that Galdós slavishly copied Feuillet. Later I shall try to show that another literary influence, *Ivanhoe*, contributed to the formation of Galdós' priests. But who can say that he did or did not know some living D. Silvestre or D. Angel? Out of the large number of priests he observed, many must have had some traits like those of his brain children. But I remain with the impression that the two Spanish priests were conceived mostly in the form and spirit of the abbé Renaud.

GLORIA AND SIBYLLE

There is a tradition,[163] as I mentioned earlier, that the model of Galdós' heroine was Juanita Lund, the daughter of the Norwegian Protestant and Spanish Catholic. This tradition is probably true with respect to the physical appearance of Gloria. Juanita was eighteen years old when Galdós saw her the summer before writing *Gloria*. From her early photographs it is evident that she was a very pretty girl of a little more than medium height, with a very straight carriage, fairly regular features, and a vitality and animation which still were evident at ninety-three, when I had the pleasure of visiting her.

In Galdós' description of Gloria he emphasizes "un espíritu de enérgica vitalidad que necesitaba emplearse constantemente," "su fisonomía, parlante y expresiva como ninguna" and "la flamígera viveza de sus ojos negros."[164] These traits could certainly reflect the living model, Juanita Lund. Gloria's mouth is a little large and her nose a little small, "pero el conjunto no podía ser más hechicero."[165] I find it impossible to state whether these remarks, which depend so much on the taste of the writer,

[163] See Berkowitz, *Pérez Galdós*, p. 146, where the circumstances by which Galdós is said to have met Juanita are incorrectly stated, although it is rightly said that she served as the model for Gloria; this tradition was confirmed orally by Dr. Gregorio Marañón.

[164] *Gloria*, p. 501 (I, 2).

[165] *Ibid.*

are descriptive of Juanita. There is no reason why they could not be Galdós' reaction to her.

In respect to up-bringing, Juanita and Gloria are worlds apart. The former's father, himself an accomplished linguist and widely read person, wanted his daughter to be well educated. He employed a young German woman trained in the Froebel system to teach her. The tutor was loved, respected, and finally mourned by the whole Lund family when she died after six years' residence in their home. Later, during excursions to Madrid, Juana met and became a friend of Francisco Giner de los Ríos and Manuel Cossío. She spoke to me of their *krausismo* and showed a general awareness of literary and philosophical currents. All this, of course, contrasts sharply with Gloria's convent education, which consisted of the catechism and church history, with smatterings of secular history, geography, astronomy, physics, and French. As regards artistic training, she embroidered fairly well and played the piano facilely but with horrible taste in music.[166]

By far the most important character trait of Gloria is her independence in thought. She astounds her family by maintaining that the expulsion of the Jews and Moriscos from Spain was wrong,[167] that the Spaniards of the seventeenth century lacked a pure morality and a simple, unsuperstitious religiosity,[168] and that man can find salvation in any religion.[169] Undoubtedly Juanita Lund also thought for herself, but in her case this trend no doubt caused pleasure rather than consternation in her family. It is necessary to turn to Sibylle in Feuillet's novel to find a situation which parallels Gloria's in this respect.

[166] *Gloria*, p. 505 (I, 5). Effie L. Erickson (*op. cit.*, p. 426) believes that the passage on Gloria's education stems from Dickens, *Dombey and Son*, Chap. XII. I find a much closer resemblance to V. Hugo, *Les misérables*, Vol. IV, Livre III, Chap. 4, where the convent education of Cosette is described: "Son éducation était terminée; c'est-à-dire on lui avait appris la religion, et même, et surtout la dévotion; puis 'l'histoire', c'est-à-dire la chose qu'on appelle ainsi au couvent, la géographie, la grammaire, les participes, les rois de France, un peu de musique, à faire un nez, etc., mais du reste elle ignorait tout, ce qui est un charme et un péril."

[167] *Gloria*, p. 505 (I, 5).

[168] *Ibid.*, p. 506 (I, 6).

[169] *Ibid.*, p. 560 (I, 30).

Sibylle starts life with a vivacious, headstrong character which is gradually curbed and brought under control. As a baby she cried desperately to possess a star which she could see out the open window from her crib;[170] as a little girl she flew into a rage because she could not ride a swan about the pond.[171] Later she kept a passionate intensity of will.[172] Gloria's father had to reprimand her for the same tendency. "Mira, hija . . . es preciso que aprendas a no ser tan vehemente, a no tomar a pechos cosas nimias y de escaso interés para el cuerpo y para el alma. ¿Cuándo te enseñaré la serenidad y el aplomo . . ."[173] This theme recurs frequently in the early part of the novel.[174] Finally, Gloria, too, brings herself under control, although not so completely as Sibylle, for Gloria's conformity is only outward. She does, however, have clipped wings and keeps her impulses to herself.[175]

The girlish impetuosity of both heroines is the motivating force of the religious doubts which both develop later. Sibylle is affected by the innocent laxity of the abbé Renaud[176] and the superstitions of her neighbors.[177] Gloria, on the other hand, is provoked to thoughts unacceptable to her neo-Catholic family, but certainly not unorthodox, by her desultory reading in her father's library.[178] Sibylle's rebellion reaches its climax when she refuses to go on preparing herself for her first communion and even gives up all practice of religion,[179] Gloria's when the bishop refuses her absolution because of her latitudinarianism.[180]

We have, to this point, the following general similarities: a very Catholic family is astounded and grieved by the discovery that a willful daughter of the family has grave doubts about some of the teachings of the church (or at least teachings of

[170] *Histoire de Sibylle*, p. 12.
[171] *Ibid.*, p. 15.
[172] *Ibid.*, p. 17.
[173] *Gloria*, p. 502 (I, 3).
[174] *Ibid.*, pp. 501 (I, 2) and 502 (I, 3).
[175] *Ibid.*, pp. 509 (I, 6) and 518 (I, 12).
[176] *Histoire de Sibylle*, pp. 72, 74, and 103.
[177] *Ibid.*, p. 85.
[178] *Gloria*, pp. 506–509 (I, 6).
[179] *Histoire de Sibylle*, p. 88.
[180] *Gloria*, p. 559 (I, 30).

the family about the church). Let us not forget that Sibylle is only twelve while Gloria is eighteen at the time the doubts develop. Thus the next general similarity, the fact that the heroine falls in love with a non-Catholic, can take place immediately for Gloria, but only after an interval of years for Sibylle. The former enters her love affair still burdened by her doubts, while the latter has already had the chance to regain her footing on the firm ground of orthodoxy.

Naturally, the contact with an admirable and lovable non-Catholic makes each of the heroines reconsider the foundations of her faith, but in Sibylle's case the decision is quickly reached,[181] while Gloria hesitates and doubts the ruling of her uncle that she cannot marry a non-Catholic. Ultimately Gloria returns to an orthodox point of view, which Sibylle has never abandoned save for her childhood doubts.

The two non-Catholic lovers have little in common, as Daniel Morton is firmly attached to his own religion while Raoul de Chalys is a declared freethinker. Yet the narrative of the two love affairs does present a certain parallelism which we shall examine immediately.

LOVE FOR A HERETIC

The usual plan for a nineteenth-century novel on religion was to portray a Catholic in love with a freethinker.[182] There is regularly an attempt on the part of the Catholic to convert the other; the freethinker is generally less moved by the proselyting spirit and is content to live in peace, with each following his own beliefs. The outcome of every religious novel is of course colored by the credences of its author: those written from the Catholic viewpoint end happily if the freethinker is converted, tragically if he is not; those whose authors are freethinkers will

[181] *Histoire de Sibylle*, p. 271.

[182] Some of the most important novels on the religious theme were Lamartine, *Raphael*; O. Feuillet, *Histoire de Sibylle* and *Monsieur de Camors*; G. Sand, *Mlle. de la Quintinie*; Galdós, *Doña Perfecta, Gloria,* and *La familia de León Roch*; Pereda, *De tal palo*; Alarcón, *El escándalo* and *El niño de la bola*; Pardo Bazán, *Un viaje de novios*; and the novels, already analyzed, by Azcárate and Villarminio.

be happy if a marriage based on mutual respect and love, without the abrogation of either partner's beliefs, is consummated, tragic if the love is thwarted by intolerance. *Gloria* belongs to this last category, but *Sibylle* is a mixed happy-tragic, Catholic novel, as the conversion of the hero is wrought only after the death of the heroine.

Despite the very different viewpoint of the two authors, they narrate the events of the two love affairs in much the same pattern. In both novels there is a long period of waiting for the predestined lover. Sibylle once saw Raoul when she was a little girl[183] and has built her recollection of him into a romantic ideal.[184] When she is about to meet Raoul again in Paris her curiosity and interest are intense. It seems that invisible hands work to keep them apart.[185] "Il lui semblait qu'elle allait voir face à face le dieu secret de sa pensée, et une sorte de trouble surnaturel envahissait son sein."[186] Raoul, on his side, has thought often of the child Sibylle, whom he has not seen for ten years.[187] As Feuillet comments: "Ces deux êtres, doués d'une imagination égale et comme inclinée dans le même sens, avaient glissé l'un vers l'autre, depuis de longues années, par une pente mystérieuse . . ."[188]

Gloria, too, has forged a romantic ideal,[189] and just before Daniel arrived at Ficóbriga she had a vivid intuition of the approaching event.[190] This sensation is intensified by Caifás' prophetic dream in which he sees her in love with a handsome but frightful man.[191]

In both novels the heroine's love starts with no knowledge of the beliefs of the man, although in each case there is the suspicion that he is not orthodox. Sibylle has never been told

[183] *Histoire de Sibylle*, p. 27.
[184] *Ibid.*, pp. 174, 229, and 241.
[185] *Ibid.*, p. 216.
[186] *Ibid.*, p. 229.
[187] *Ibid.*, p. 244.
[188] *Ibid.*, p. 251.
[189] *Gloria*, p. 518 (I, 12).
[190] *Ibid.*, pp. 520–521 (I, 14).
[191] *Ibid.*, p. 524 (I, 15).

anything about Raoul's principles. She knows that most men of her social group are incredulous, but she assumes that such a noble and superior person as Raoul must be a believer.[192] Gloria's family assumes that Daniel must be a Protestant since he comes from England.[193] Gloria herself is astounded to hear them say so and urges her uncle to work toward Morton's conversion.[194]

At this point Galdós has telescoped the two conversions of Feuillet's novel into one. Gloria's attitude toward Daniel's supposed Protestantism corresponds to Sibylle's toward the newly engaged tutor, Miss O'Neil. The latter reveals herself as a Protestant on the day of her arrival, striking the family with consternation[195] and causing Sibylle to urge the curé to undertake her conversion.[196] Later the knowledge of Daniel's real creed, Judaism, bursts upon Gloria as a shock from which she can never wholly recover, just as Sibylle, having heard that Raoul is an atheist, faints away and begins a decline which ultimately results in her death.[197] Neither heroine wishes to see her lover again;[198] in neither case is there any question of attempting a conversion of the man until the family intervenes in his favor in hopes of reaching a solution which would bring happiness to their daughter.[199]

Although the girl in each case is firm in her resolve not to marry a nonbeliever,[200] she is still fatally drawn to the man.[201] Both men have originally declared that they cannot pretend to have a faith they do not really feel.[202] Both think that love is a more important binding force than religion.[203] The progress

[192] *Histoire de Sibylle*, p. 246.
[193] *Gloria*, p. 532 (I, 20).
[194] *Ibid.*, p. 534 (I, 20).
[195] *Histoire de Sibylle*, p. 49.
[196] *Ibid.*, p. 57.
[197] *Histoire de Sibylle*, p. 270.
[198] *Ibid.*, p. 271; *Gloria*, pp. 616 (II, 11) and 627 (II, 15).
[199] *Histoire de Sibylle*, p. 318; *Gloria*, p. 611 (II, 11).
[200] *Histoire de Sibylle*, p. 179; *Gloria*, pp. 579 (I, 37) and 627 (II, 16).
[201] *Histoire de Sibylle*, pp. 279 and 285; *Gloria*, p. 674 (II, 32).
[202] *Histoire de Sibylle*, p. 271; *Gloria*, p. 614 (II, 11).
[203] *Histoire de Sibylle*, p. 371; *Gloria*, p. 578 (I, 37).

toward a conversion is slow. There is a gleam of hope when Raoul begins to feel the faith inherent in the simple country existence of Férias,[204] which sentiment corresponds to the announcement of Daniel's impending conversion. Yet the hope is dashed as Raoul's atheism is reaffirmed by the death of his friend Gandax,[205] and Daniel's mother prevents his feigned conversion.[206]

The final scenes of both works show considerable parallelism. Both heroines are already emotionally shattered by the intensity of their situations; both are greatly weakened by a long walk at night;[207] both die in a building next to a village church.[208] Each one feels that her death is a sacrifice by which she brings her lover to the true faith,[209] for in each case there is a scene in which the lover gives signs of conversion,[210] although in Daniel's case it is only pretended to spare the dying Gloria additional pain.[211] Both women die giving the name of husband to their lovers[212] and with the conviction that they will be united with them in paradise.[213]

No one would admit more readily than I that an immense number of details in both accounts are different, as was indeed required by the different accessory characters, the different settings, and the radically different points of view of the two authors. There are no verbal parallels or direct copying. Yet there does remain an essential stream of narrative which is truly alike and which becomes really significant when considered in conjunction with the shipwreck scene, where we saw incontrovertible evidence of Galdós' drawing upon *Sibylle.*

There are also some minor characters who are related to the two heroines in similar fashion. Sibylle has made Jacques Feray, the village fool, her favorite charity and received a doglike

[204] *Histoire de Sibylle,* p. 342.
[205] *Ibid.,* p. 365.
[206] *Gloria,* p. 661 (II, 29).
[207] *Histoire de Sibylle,* pp. 373–375; *Gloria,* p. 669 (II, 31).
[208] *Histoire de Sibylle,* p. 381; *Gloria,* p. 670 (II, 31).
[209] *Histoire de Sibylle,* p. 331; *Gloria,* pp. 674 and 676 (II, 32).
[210] *Histoire de Sibylle,* pp. 379 and 385.
[211] *Gloria,* p. 676 (II, 32).
[212] *Histoire de Sibylle,* p. 386; *Gloria,* p. 675 (II, 32).
[213] *Histoire de Sibylle,* p. 386; *Gloria,* p. 676 (II, 32).

fidelity and admiration in exchange.[214] Raoul secretly provides Jacques with a sum of money for preserving intact the tombs of his wife and daughter.[215] Gloria's favorite charity is Caifás, the village sexton and ne'er-do-well,[216] and Daniel secretly gives a large sum of money to Caifás to get him out of the hands of a usurer.[217] Of course the effect of both these donations, which ultimately become known to all, is to increase the admiration of the heroine for the hero.

Furthermore, each young woman has an official suitor before the appearance of the hero, and in each case the candidate is supposed to be the paragon of Catholic gentlemen. Sibylle's candidate, the Baron de Val-Chesnay, is proposed by no less a person than the bishop of the diocese[218] and has the full approbation of her family.[219] In much the same way Rafael del Horro, the pretender to Gloria's hand, comes to Ficóbriga with the bishop, D. Angel,[220] who presents him to Gloria's family as the "benemérito campeón de los buenos principios, de las creencias religiosas, de la iglesia católica . . ."[221] Gloria's father is wholly in favor of the union.[222] Yet both these suitors are treated in a humorous vein by their creators, and both fail in their pretensions. The two men show no great similarities to each other, aside from being pompous and self-satisfied, but we are struck by their function as pendants to the two heroines and contrasts to the heroes.

All things considered, we conclude that Galdós had a detailed recollection of the *Histoire de Sibylle* in mind when the plan of *Gloria* broke upon him. But he rejected much of it, combined or divided characters, and altered situations to fit his liberal point of view. In short, he used the French novel only as raw material,

[214] *Histoire de Sibylle*, pp. 33–34.
[215] *Ibid.*, p. 336.
[216] *Gloria*, pp. 522 (I, 15) and 548 (I, 25).
[217] *Ibid.*, p. 549 (I, 25).
[218] *Histoire de Sibylle*, p. 141.
[219] *Ibid.*, p. 143.
[220] *Gloria*, p. 511 (I, 8).
[221] *Ibid.*, p. 512 (I, 9).
[222] *Ibid.*, p. 515 (I, 11).

just as he used the philosophy, the real people, and places he knew in various combinations.

It may be that, without realizing what he was doing, Galdós allowed certain reminiscences of Feuillet's novel to creep into *Gloria.* This would be the most charitable view of Galdós' borrowings, according to the generally held notions on "originality" and "creative imagination." On the other hand, Don Benito may have deliberately read or reread his copy of *Sibylle* – knowing that it dealt with the religious theme – with the specific purpose of finding material he could utilize in a projected novel on religion. This last possibility might bring the word "plagiarism" to mind. Yet, despite the ugly implication, I feel that that is exactly what Galdós did, as I shall try to demonstrate in the following pages. Later on, I shall try to show why we should not regard the borrowing of suggestions from literary models in a much different light from borrowing from living ones.

THE BIBLE AND A BANQUET

In *Gloria* Galdós cites the Bible more than forty times. For example, in the second part, when he wants to make Daniel's servant into a second Sancho Panza, he has him quote many proverbs.[223] Sansón is a Jew, so the sayings are taken, not from the popular knowledge of the Spanish people, as in Sancho's case, but from the Bible, especially Proverbs and Ecclesiastes.

In other places, the Biblical material is used in quite a different way. Almost the first thing Daniel says after his rescue is "¡Señor, Señor nuestro! ¡cuán maravilloso es tu nombre en toda la tierra!"[224] Instantly the bishop, Don Angel, repeats the same quotation in Latin. A little later, as the conversation draws to a close, Daniel again cites a verse from the Bible which the bishop gives in its Latin form.[225]

[223] *Gloria,* p. 624 (II, 15), where Sansón quotes from Ecclesiastes 11:10 and 1:14 and Proverbs 7:22–23 and 7:7–11; *Gloria,* p. 625 (II, 15), where Sansón quotes Proverbs 27:12, 22:14, and 23:27; *Gloria,* p. 626 (II, 15), where he cites Ecclesiastes 1:2–4 and 1:9–10.

[224] *Gloria,* p. 531 (I, 19); *cf.* Psalms 8:10.

[225] *Gloria,* p. 532 (I, 19); *cf.* Proverbs 21:21.

The intent of these quotations could not be clearer. It is Galdós' way to telling us from the very beginning that the bishop and the stranger are fundamentally one in their religion. Each one uses the same words to glorify the same God. At least the essence of their religion is the same. Later, in the second part, during the celebrations of Holy Week, the quotations from church liturgy are all those which are derived directly from the Old Testament, proving again the close relationship of Judaism and Catholicism.[226]

Now in Don Benito's library there is a Bible giving both the Spanish and Latin texts in parallel columns.[227] Galdós marked eleven passages in the Psalms and Proverbs (but nothing else), among them the two verses just cited by both Daniel and Don Angel.[228] Furthermore, four other marked passages are quoted elsewhere in the first part of *Gloria.* In addition a large number of other phrases are taken from the Psalms and Proverbs near, although not actually in, the marked passages. In some cases both the Latin and Spanish texts appear in the novel. There can be no question that Galdós used this Bible to document himself while preparing *Gloria.*

One passage from the Psalms is of special significance. Don Silvestre Romero has planned a great banquet to celebrate the political victory of the *neocatólicos* in the recent elections. The only important person in Ficóbriga who refuses to take part is the spiritual and unpolitical Don Angel. The parish priest tries to persuade him to change his mind, saying: "¿Se trata por ventura de una orgía? El salmista ha dicho: 'Banqueteen los justos.' *Et justi epulentur.—Et justi epulentur et exultent in conspectu Dei*—añadió vivamente el Prelado.—'Y regocíjense en la pre-

[226] *Gloria,* p. 596 (II, 6), where there are citations from Exodus 15:27 and 16:4; also *Gloria,* p. 640 (II, 21), which cites Psalms 68:2–4 and 68:6; and Lamentations 1:1–2.

[227] *La Santa Biblia* (traducida al español . . . por el ilmo. Sr. D. Felipe Scio de S. Miguel . . .), Gaspar y Roig, Madrid, 1852.

[228] The marked passages are in Psalms 8:7–10, 13:1–4, 34:2–3, 67:1–5, 76:20, 103:24, and 117:16; and in Proverbs 19:13, 21:13, 21:21, 22:9, and 25:22. (The numberings given here follow the Vulgate and Spanish Bibles, which differ from those of the English and Hebrew texts.)

sencia de Dios.' No violentemos los sagrados textos, señor cura . . ." [229]

In his Bible, Galdós marked not only the words he utilized but the first five verses of the Psalm. In the Spanish version they read:

1. Salmo de cántico al mismo David.

2. Levántese Dios, y sean dispersos sus enemigos, y huyan de su presencia, los que le aborrecen.

3. Como se desvanece el humo, así se desvanezcan: como se derrite la cera delante del fuego, así perezcan los pecadores delante de Dios.

4. Y los justos banqueteen, y regocíjense en la presencia de Dios, y deléitense en alegría.

5. Cantad a Dios, salmead al nombre de él: aparejad el camino a aquél, que sube sobre el Occidente: su nombre es Señor.[230]

This Biblical passage represents the chosen few exulting over the destruction of the wicked, precisely the spirit of the neo-Catholic banquet in *Gloria* celebrating the political defeat of the liberals, or in neo-Catholic terminology, the enemies of God.

After eating well and not without sensuality, Don Silvestre Romero speaks to the group. His remarks give the tone of the whole gathering: "Hemos combatido como buenos . . . En los libros santos se ha dicho: 'Y tú, Jehová, Dios de los ejércitos, no hayas misericordia de los que se rebelan con iniquidad . . . Acábalos con furor, acábalos, y no sean; y sepan que Dios domina en Jacob hasta los confines de la tierra.' [231] Y en otro paisaje: 'Fuego irá delante de él y abrasará en redor sus enemigos.' [232] Nuestra obligación es pues, combatir . . ." [233] The same line of thought is continued in the speech of Rafael del Horro, who urges the guests to be strong in war for the defense of the church and to combat the nefarious "espíritu moderno." Especially he decries the present situation of the pope, a prisoner in the Vatican.[234]

[229] *Gloria*, pp. 564–565 (I, 32).
[230] Psalms 67:1–5.
[231] Psalms 58:6 and 58:14.
[232] Psalms 96:3.
[233] *Gloria*, p. 567 (I, 33).
[234] *Ibid.*, pp. 567–568 (I, 33).

The reason why the neo-Catholic orators can quote so aptly from the Bible is that they cite passages in which God is still the early Jewish tribal deity, now leading his chosen people to the destruction of their neighbors, now wrathfully punishing them for running after other gods. He is still the god who dwells on Mount Sinai and in the temple, not He who has the starry heavens for His throne and the earth for His footstool. Galdós saw that neo-Catholicism and primitive Judaism were identical in spirit. Here we come back to the very kernel of *Gloria* – two fanaticisms, two intolerances, essentially the same in quality and wholly opposed to the spirit of religion, which Galdós is going to put into conflict with each other.

It is now important for us to determine when Galdós sought and marked the passages in his Bible which he was to use in *Gloria*. The quotation which introduces the banquet sheds some significant light on the subject. Don Rafael and Don Silvestre were already presented as politicians at their first appearance near the beginning of the novel.[235] And precisely at this place Silvestre Romero quotes, in both Latin and Spanish, the two verses of the Psalms which immediately precede the allusion to the banquet of the righteous: "Levántese Dios y sean dispersos sus enemigos, y huyan . . . Como se derrite la cera delante del fuego, así perezcan los pecadores delante de Dios."[236] Galdós had, then, already marked these verses and the one which follows, alluding to the banquet, by the time he was starting to write the novel.

But even more is implied. At the moment that the politicians are introduced as such, Galdós has already planned their triumph and the banquet which is to celebrate it. Since he read and marked the Bible before writing the book, it must follow almost surely that he got the suggestion of the banquet from the Biblical passage so closely connected with it. We can hardly suppose that he first imagined a banquet, and then, searching more or less at random in his Bible, had the extreme good fortune to

[235] *Gloria*, p. 513 (I, 9).
[236] *Ibid.*; *cf.* Psalms 67:2–3.

find a passage exactly suited to the tone of the gathering he had already conceived.

It is clear, then, that Galdós had the political action and the resultant banquet in mind *even as he began to write the book,* that in all probability he planned it on the suggestion of the passage in the Psalms, and that he must have been reading and marking part of his Bible with the definite purpose of seeking out materials for his new book.

But I think we can put the time of the reading and marking of the Bible even earlier, before the inspired moment in the Puerta del Sol when the plan of the whole first part of *Gloria* occurred to him. In the first place, Galdós says that in the Puerta del Sol he saw "con claridad toda la primera parte." [237] The banquet and the political campaign were part of this vision, as they were an important element in the plan of the first part. But he could hardly have envisioned the banquet without having first known the passage from the Psalms; therefore he must have read and marked the Bible even before the moment of inspiration. Galdós was not waiting for inspiration but going out to meet it. He already had a general notion of what kind of a book he intended to write and was collecting materials which would help him in producing it.

An examination of the other marked Biblical passages leads to the same conclusion. Galdós marked eleven passages from which he used but five – one of them in two different places in the novel. If the detailed plan of the book had already flashed upon him, he would have marked only those which he needed. Some of the unused passages are quite different from the neo-Catholic spirit, and could hardly be used in the book as we have it. Then, the many additional quotations from the Psalms which are *not* marked in the Bible indicate that later, once the writing was under way, he ran down vaguely remembered passages (which he could not have remembered accurately both in the Latin and Spanish versions) and transferred them immediately to his manuscript, not bothering to mark them in in the

[237] L. Alas (Clarín), *Galdós,* p. 28.

Bible since they were not for future use. From this we can argue that the marked passages were designated certainly before the idea of *Gloria* had taken final form.

We have taken an important step in our understanding of Galdós' creative process. He was deliberately reading with the idea of collecting material for a book, and this search took place before the moment of inspiration when the raw material fell into a pattern and was then rapidly transferred to paper. We immediately suspect that the suggestion of the banquet was a fortuitous find and that the real purpose of the search through the Psalms was to find material on the Jews. Galdós must, then, have had already the idea of a Jewish hero.

This is also suggested by the fact that Galdós read attentively the long article on the "Hebreos" in his encyclopedia.[238] In the section called "Poesía de los Hebreos," where many examples of beautiful poetry from the Old Testament are given, he marked six long passages, no part of which appears in *Gloria*. Obviously, he could have read this work at any time in his mature life, yet it is plausible to assume that he grounded himself in Jewish matters before writing about a Jewish hero. There is abundant evidence that he frequently used his encyclopedia as a source of factual information.[239]

But if he read and marked this article on the Jews as a preparation for *Gloria*, he did so at a stage when the idea was much vaguer than when he read the Psalms, for if the concept of the novel had been precise he would have marked in the poetry at least some things relating to it, or else nothing at all. I surmise that he turned first to the encyclopedia for information on the

[238] Francisco de P. Mellado, *Enciclopedia moderna . . .*, Madrid, 1853, Vol. 22. The marked passages on Biblical poetry are found in cols. 664–672.

[239] Galdós used his encyclopedia constantly for information on factual matters. For example, the article on "croup" is marked, certainly as preparation for writing the description of the sickness in *La familia de León Roch*, Part II, Chap. 4. This novel was written in 1878. Earlier, in 1874, *Juan Martín el Empecinado* pictured the life of the *Guerrilleros*, and we find many marks in the article called "Guerrillero" in the encyclopedia, Vol. 22, cols. 236–248. The unquestionable dependence of these works on the encyclopedia, just before and after the novel which interests us, makes it seem credible that Galdós sought information in the same source for *Gloria*.

Jews, and that it called his attention to the beauty of Biblical poetry and was the immediate cause of his reading the Psalms.

On another page of *Gloria*, Galdós quotes the Psalmist in his description of a great tempest.[240] In his Bible, only the last verse of this passage is marked: "En la mar fué tu camino, y tus sendas en las muchas aguas, y tus pisadas no fueron conocidas." This suggests that at the time he marked his Bible the idea of a shipwreck was already in Don Benito's mind, unless the Bible itself gave the idea to him. But if the shipwreck occurred to him on or before reading the Psalms, he must have already localized his novel on the seacoast. Then since the plan of the shipwreck (as we have it) is inseparable from Feuillet's *Histoire de Sibylle*, we can suppose that he had already read this work. In addition, the localization on the coast brings us inevitably back to Galdós' friends in Santander in whose spirit the Lantigua family was created.

In short, I think that he had already chosen many elements of his story before the moment of crystallization. What is especially important is that this material was gathered systematically and with the deliberate purpose of constructing a novel. The only problem Galdós had left was the proper selection and arrangement of material, and this was what occurred to him in the Puerta del Sol.

Pierre Audiat, in his valuable study of literary creation, lays down a rule which is applicable here. "*L'idée génératrice apparaît brusquement*," he says, but adds, "Que le mot *brusquement* ne fasse pas illusion. Dire que l'idée génératrice apparaît brusquement n'est pas affirmer que rien ne l'a préparée. Au contraire; si, en certains cas, l'apparition de l'idée est aussi inattendue qu'imprévisible, dans beaucoup d'autres elle est attendue, désirée; il y a eu incubation de longue durée ou volonté de la voir surgir. Mais dans tous les cas, il semble que le moment décisif de l'invention soit une illumination brève, où l'inventeur aperçoit

[240] *Gloria*, p. 572 (I, 35), where Galdós quotes Psalms 76:17–20. In his Bible he marked only Psalms 76:20. Later, in the second part, Chap. 30, "La visión del hombre sobre las aguas," is also partly inspired by this same passage.

ce qu'il n'avait pas aperçu auparavant."[241] This observation, based on the statements of many authors, is also valid for Galdós if we see the moment of crystallization of *Gloria* not as the inception of the work but rather as the end of a fairly long period of incubation.

Among the preparatory reading for *Gloria* there must have been a certain number of books on the religious problem in general, of which Feuillet's *Histoire de Sibylle* would be one. But in my opinion, the most important part of Galdós' preparation was the reading or rereading of books of Jewish interest. Obviously this was the element in the novel about which he had the least information. My belief is that he deliberately turned to the Bible, Heine, Spinoza, Sue, perhaps Lessing's *Nathan the Wise*, and Scott's *Ivanhoe* as the literary men and works then universally associated with the Jews. It is difficult to prove this assertion in every case, but if we can establish its truth in at least one instance besides the Bible, the plausibility of the other cases will be greatly enhanced. We shall begin with *Ivanhoe*.

IVANHOE

When Gloria looks for something interesting to read in her father's library she discovers a copy of *Ivanhoe*.[242] Don Juan admits that it is a good novel, but advises his daughter not to read it yet. Instead he suggests that she read some of the thoroughly Catholic authors – Chateaubriand, Bernardin de St. Pierre, and especially Manzoni. At this early point in *Gloria*, Galdós, who wants to name a novel more or less at random, chooses *Ivanhoe*. Of course he wishes a novel which contrasts with the neo-Catholic spirit, but there are hundreds of possibilities. That Galdós selected *Ivanhoe* was no doubt because he remembered its Jewish characters, Isaac of York and Rebecca, and because he was himself beginning a work with a Jewish hero.

[241] Pierre Audiat, *La biographie de l'oeuvre littéraire – Esquisse d'une méthode critique*, Paris, 1924, pp. 116–117.

[242] *Gloria*, p. 505 (I, 5). *Ivanhoe* is the only modern novel named in *Gloria*.

This in itself would not suffice to show that Don Benito had *recently* gone through Scott's novel. But that he had read this novel, which enjoyed such great popularity in Spain, must be evident from his already cited knowledge of its anticlerical tone and Jewish characters. It would be easy to accumulate evidence that Galdós thought highly of Scott, whom he mentions with approbation many times. In his personal library he had the complete works of Scott,[243] but the copy of *Ivanhoe* is not marked. Thus while we can say that he admired Scott, that he must have read *Ivanhoe*, and that he remembered it as he began *Gloria*, we cannot yet argue that he reread *Ivanhoe* as a partial preparation for his own novel.

But as his novel proceeds, Galdós has occasion to name an English ship. Out of the thousands of possibilities, he selects the word *Plantagenet*.[244] In the last quarter of *Ivanhoe*, Richard Coeur-de-Lion is repeatedly called "Richard Plantagenet."[245] In all probability the name of the ship was taken from the English novel which Galdós mentioned not long before. But the remembrance of a detail like this implies a recent perusal of Scott's work. We have, then, reason to presume that *Ivanhoe* was part of Galdós' preparatory reading for *Gloria*.

This same impression becomes very much stronger when we turn our attention to a comparison between Prior Aymer and Silvestre Romero. We have already seen that the latter was a priest famed for his prowess in the hunt and at the trencher. Scott presents to us his worldly monk, Prior Aymer, with these words: ". . . the Prior of Jorvaulx Abbey, well known for many miles around as a lover of the chase, of the banquet, and, if fame did him not wrong, of other worldly pleasures . . ."[246] Scott goes on to tell us that Aymer enjoyed a high opinion among the nobility because of "his free and jovial temper" and

[243] The Handy-Volume "Scott" Edition of Sir Walter Scott's Works, London, n.d., 31 vols., vol. 17 missing.

[244] *Gloria*, p. 526 (I, 17).

[245] W. Scott, *Ivanhoe*, Leipzig, B. Tauchnitz, 1845, pp. 408, 498, 499, 514, 521, and 539.

[246] *Ibid*., p. 45.

that he was highly regarded by the common people because of his generous charity.[247]

This corresponds to what Galdós says of Romero, who was "muy alegre, muy rumboso, vivísimo de ingenio, generoso, y de trato galán y campechano con grandes y pequeños . . . Socorría benigno a los menesterosos, se preciaba de hacer muchas limosnas, y por esto, así como por su carácter franco y bondadoso, estaba muy en paz con sus feligreses." [248]

But in this passage Galdós has attributed to the parish priest certain traits which he denies him elsewhere. For example, his keenness of wit ("vivísimo de ingenio") abandons him when he welcomes Don Angel [249] and again when he speaks at the banquet, at which time Don Juan's mental comment is "Más vale que te calles, pedazo de alcornoque."[250] In his conversation with Rafael del Horro he shows simplicity and even stupidity rather than brilliance.[251] On the other hand Prior Aymer's sparkling sayings are one of his outstanding characteristics. Another case in point is Romero's generosity and charity. His dismissal of Caifás from the sexton's position [252] contrasts with Gloria's, Don Angel's, and Daniel's charity toward the same person.

Finally another change in conception appears when Galdós makes Romero first a wealthy man who "poseía regular hacienda heredada,"[253] and then makes him embrace the priesthood on parental advice in order to get the income from certain chaplain's positions.[254] The implication is that the family is first well-to-do as in the case of Prior Aymer, and then of poor peasant stock, like that of l'abbé Renaud.

I have already noted an artistic incongruity in Don Silvestre's character and ascribed it to the unskillful blending of source materials. I have the same impression with respect to the incon-

[247] *Ibid.*, p. 46.
[248] *Gloria*, p. 528 (I, 18).
[249] *Ibid.*, p. 512 (I, 9).
[250] *Ibid.*, p. 567 (I, 33).
[251] *Ibid.*, pp. 537–538 (I, 21).
[252] *Ibid.*, p. 523 (I, 15).
[253] *Ibid.*, p. 528 (I, 18).
[254] *Ibid.*, p. 529 (I, 18).

sistencies we have just noted. I did not originally stress the most obvious similarities in the two clergymen – their love of hunting and banqueting – as these are common conditions in all "jolly friars." But now that the two men seem to be related on different grounds, it becomes probable that Romero's devotion to the chase and to food has its origin in Prior Aymer. Having made him a hunter and an inhabitant of la Montaña, Galdós immediately associates him with Los Picos de Europa, the hunter's paradise within the province, which Don Benito had visited only a short time before he wrote *Gloria*.[255]

Besides these specific relations between *Ivanhoe* and *Gloria*, there are certain vaguer resemblances between the two novels. In the first place, there are a number of general ideas common to both works. Scott points out five times that the God of the Christians and the Jews is the same;[256] we have already seen that this idea underlies *Gloria*. Then the Jews of the two novels, although greatly differentiated by the centuries which separate them, have nonetheless some elements in common. They are wealthy, their homes are luxurious, their wealth is important to the state and indispensable to the upper classes.[257] They of course quote or allude constantly to the Bible.[258] They yearn for the lost Zion, a country of their own.[259] Finally the feeling against them in both novels is such that even a noble spirit cannot completely overcome his prejudices against them.[260]

In *Ivanhoe* Scott takes the Order of the Temple as his whipping boy and makes it exemplify ecclesiastical laxness (in Bois-Guilbert), hypocrisy (in Albert Malvoisin of Templestowe and Conrade Mont-Fichet), and puritanical fanaticism (in the Grand Master Lucas Beaumanoir). Galdós studies hypocrisy in the person of Don Buenaventura, exaggerated puritanism in Doña

[255] *Cuarenta leguas*, in *Obras completas*, Aguilar, VI, 1506.
[256] *Ivanhoe*, pp. 90, 228, 330, 452, and 550.
[257] *Ibid.*, pp. 141–142 and 326; *Gloria*, p. 653 (II, 26).
[258] *Ivanhoe*, pp. 89, 95, 132, etc.; part of Daniel's Biblical quotations have been listed in notes 224, 225, and 240 of this chapter, but this is only a small part of the total. Sansón's use of the Bible is shown in note 223.
[259] *Ivanhoe*, p. 452; *Gloria*, pp. 615 (II, 11) and 653 (II, 26).
[260] *Ivanhoe*, p. 328; *Gloria*, p. 576 (I, 37).

Serafinita, and a moderate character with just the germ of fanaticism in Don Juan. Let us see what suggestions he could have found in *Ivanhoe* for these characters.

In Scott's novel, hypocrisy would not be an important theme, were it not for the growing fanaticism of the Order[261] which caused those who acted or thought differently from the exact letter of the law to conceal their deeds and thoughts. In the Spanish situation the hypocrites act either from self-interest, in order to have the support of a solid, powerful minority group (for example, Rafael del Horro) or because they do not wish to upset the established order (for example, Don Buenaventura). The latter is actually a rationalist at heart.[262] His confession of faith shows him to be almost a *krausista,* the only difference being that he will not openly avow his beliefs. His policy becomes one of saving appearances, of suggesting and accepting a conversion with mental reservations.[263]

This is the same spirit revealed by the Christian knight, Mont-Fichet, when he says of Rebecca "it were better that this miserable damsel die, than that Brian de Bois-Guilbert should be lost to the Order, or the Order divided by internal dissension."[264] Following this policy, Mont-Fichet and Albert Malvoisin of Templestowe (who "knew how to throw over his vices and his ambition the veil of hypocrisy, and to assume in his exterior the fanaticism which he internally despised")[265] proceeded to bribe witnesses to testify against Rebecca. By the sacrifice of her life they hoped to save appearances for the Order.

Later Bois-Guilbert shows that he too detests the fanaticism of the Grand Master: "Could I guess the unexpected arrival of yon dotard, whom some flashes of frantic valour, and the praises yielded by fools to stupid self-torments of an ascetic, have raised for the present above his own merits, above common sense, above me, and above the hundreds of our Order, who think and feel

[261] *Ivanhoe,* p. 419.
[262] *Gloria,* p. 613 (II, 11).
[263] *Ibid.,* p. 618 (II, 12).
[264] *Ivanhoe,* p. 437.
[265] *Ibid.,* p. 430.

as men free from such silly and fantastic prejudices as are the grounds of his opinions and actions?" [266]

He suggests that Rebecca flee with him to a freer atmosphere, even if it involves fighting against his own Order: "We will go to Palestine, where Conrade, Marquis of Monserrat, is my friend – a friend free as myself from the doting scruples which fetter our freeborn reason – rather with Saladin will we league ourselves, than endure the scorn of bigots whom we contemn." [267]

While these rebellious exclamations of Bois-Guilbert show the underlying disbelief in strict adherence to the letter of the law, they differ greatly from the hypocritical conformity we saw in Mont-Fichet and Albert Malvoisin. All these pictures of rationalists within the ranks of fanaticism may have helped fix in Galdós' mind the character of Don Buenaventura, although surely the latter's hypocrisy and willingness to sacrifice others to save appearances would be suggested only by Mont-Fichet and Malvoisin.

In Lucas Beaumanoir we see a man "in whose mind the suppression of each feeling of humanity which could interfere with his imagined duty was a virtue of itself." [268] He proceeds to the trial of Rebecca in this spirit, putting aside all humanitarian impulses and adhering only to the exact letter of the law. This is precisely the spirit in which Doña Serafinita tried to force Gloria to renounce her child and enter the convent. She was "el alma de más rectitud que podía existir, y si hubiera destruído al género humano, Dios se lo perdonaría, porque sin duda lo habría hecho por convicción y creyendo que realizaba un bien. . . . Y sin embargo, el alma tan limpia de perversidad podía ser dañosa . . . ¡Lástima grande que aquella santidad no fuese más humana!" [269] Here again there is a possible suggestion of a Galdosian character in *Ivanhoe*.

To my mind a closer parallel exists between the speech of Beaumanoir, deploring the decadence of the Temple, and Don

[266] *Ibid.*, p. 467.
[267] *Ibid.*, p. 471.
[268] *Ibid.*, p. 449.
[269] *Gloria*, p. 640 (II, 21).

Juan de Lantigua's speech at the banquet, decrying the worldliness and lack of faith in Spain. Both orators urge a return to primitive virtue. Each one calls for an awakening of the faithful, a return to the "sobriety, self-devotion, and piety of our predecessors" [270] or "abnegación, paciencia, martirio." [271]

The Templar predicts that, without inward reform, "the Order of the Temple will be utterly demolished – and the place thereof shall no more be known among the nations," [272] corresponding to Don Juan's earlier prophecies of dispersion, slavery, and destruction of Spain in the fires of Nineveh.[273] The Grand Master calls for a renunciation of "our ease, our comforts, and our natural affections" [274] as Don Juan declares that he would sacrifice for a return to his concept of religion "cuanto poseo, la paz de mi familia, mi familia misma, mi persona miserable." [275] Both speakers oppose to the warlike aggressiveness of their followers their belief that inward purity, good example, and prayer are more efficacious than swords.

It would be folly to maintain that one of these speeches was modeled on the other, in the narrow sense of the word "modeled." Yet it is wholly possible that the suggestion of Don Juan's speech, contrasting in tone to the bellicose utterances of Don Silvestre, came from *Ivanhoe*. In Beaumanoir, Galdós could not help noting the prophetic spirit, which he appropriated for his character and reinforced by his Biblical readings. Thus he calls Don Juan "un nuevo Isaías" in his first analysis of his personality [276] and, as we have just seen, makes him prophesy calamities to Spain. Later, when the dishonor of his daughter's sin falls upon Don Juan, Galdós, carrying on the Biblical associations, sees him as Job and twice cites passages from the book of Job to reinforce this impression.[277]

[270] *Ivanhoe*, p. 432.
[271] *Gloria*, p. 568 (I, 33).
[272] *Ivanhoe*, p. 432.
[273] *Gloria*, p. 512 (I, 9).
[274] *Ivanhoe*, p. 424.
[275] *Gloria*, p. 568 (I, 33).
[276] *Ibid.*, p. 504 (I, 4).
[277] *Ibid.*, pp. 580 and 581 (I, 38). The chapter title is "Job."

The sequence of steps in the creation of Don Juan de Lantigua must have conformed more or less to the following pattern: Over several years Galdós had been visiting Pereda and other similar neo-Catholic friends in Santander. Don Benito had had many discussions with Pereda on literary, social, and political subjects, which we can take to be typical of his relations with neo-Catholics. Sometimes the fraternal harmony of their souls was apparent, sometimes the profound division between them. At times the disputes became lively, and Galdós made concessions to his friend's beliefs. But "Pereda no cedía nunca. Es irreductible, homogéneo, y de una consistencia que excluye toda disgregación."[278]

This delightful companion, with only a germ of intolerance, probably became associated, consciously or subconsciously, with Beaumanoir. This took place when Galdós turned to *Ivanhoe* and other books of Jewish subjects in order to document himself for his new novel. At the same time he pursued rather extensive readings in the Old Testament. The prophetic tone of Beaumanoir led to an association of Don Juan with the Old Testament prophets, particularly Isaiah. Then his misfortunes brought on the comparison to Job. Nevertheless, I believe that the living model is by far the most important ingredient in this composite character.

In this discussion we have established certain facts pertinent to our study of the workings of Galdós' creative mind. We can say that he was planning a novel with a Jewish hero some time before the work took form in the Puerta del Sol. He was preparing himself for this work by systematic readings which had to do with the Jews. It is almost certain that he read *Ivanhoe* for this reason, although from it he took, not suggestions for his Jewish characters, but rather traits of his neo-Catholic personages. In a moment we shall see that he also probably read the works of Heine and Auerbach's *Benito Espinosa* and from them derived ideas for his Jewish hero.

[278] *Discursos leídos ante la Real Academia Española . . . el 7 y 21 de febrero de 1897*, p. 153.

The glorious Revolution of 1868 was the triumph of Galdós' political party. The *progresistas* speedily took up the question of religious reform and wrote an article into the new constitution which proclaimed complete liberty of conscience. This was interpreted to mean that the Jews were now free to return to Spain and that the expulsion of 1492 was finally revoked.[279] The *progresistas* copied with admiration the British plan of government; hence it is possible that the complete enfranchisement of the English Jews, which ended with the seating of Baron Rothschild in Parliament (1852), had some effect on the Spanish party and its orators. Young Benito Pérez Galdós, who covered the sessions of the Cortes Constituyentes for his newspaper, thrilled to the speeches in favor of tolerance.[280]

We can, I am sure, take it for granted that Galdós warmed not only to religious tolerance in general but also to sympathy for the Jews in particular. In his personal library there are a considerable number of books showing his interest in the Jews, and often their markings indicate clearly that Galdós opposed the original expulsion and the subsequent harsh treatment of the *conversos* who remained in Spain.[281]

Then there are a number of sympathetically treated Jews in Don Benito's works. In his early description of Toledo (1870) he enumerates among the racial types once found in the Imperial

[279] J. Amador de los Ríos, *Historia de los judíos de España y Portugal*, Madrid, 1875, III, 561–568. See also H. Graetz, *Les Juifs d'Espagne*, Paris, 1872, p. 432: "Aujourd'hui l'Espagne cherche à réparer à la fois les fautes et les injustices du passé; dejà elle vient de rouvrir ses portes aux exilés de 1492. C'est un premier pas dans la voie du progrès résolûment adoptée par un gouvernement sagement libérale . . ."

[280] See p. 39 of this volume, n. 78.

[281] In the *Obras póstumas de Moratín*, Madrid, 1867, II, 87, he marked a letter describing a synagogue in the Papal States and recommending to Spaniards the same tolerance found in the pope. He possessed and marked the work *Orden de Ros Asanah y Kypvr* (traduzido en Español, y de nuevo emmendado, y añadido el Keter Malchut y otras cosas, Amsterdam, en casa de Joris Trigg, A. 5412), to which specific book Galdós may allude in *Gloria* when he says that the Spanish Israelites "leen sus oraciones en los libros rabínicos impresos en nuestro idioma" (*Gloria*, p. 653; II, 26). Several other items could be added to this list.

City "el judío, grave, hermoso, pálido, con la barba bermeja y partida . . ."[282] Later he gives us Almudena (*Misericordia*, 1897), who, though an Arab by race, is a Jew by religion. He also presents us with a whole group of Sephardim in *Aitta Tetauen* (1904–1905). We are not surprised to learn from his *Memorias* that his visit to the ghetto in Amsterdam interested him greatly.[283] Finally, the small number of Jewish financiers and merchants who had established themselves in Madrid despite the official lack of tolerance – the Weisweillers, Bauers, Rosenthals, and Bachs[284] – are named in a number of Galdós' works. Don Benito calls the most notable Jewish banker (to whom we shall return soon) "el simpático y bondadoso don Ignacio."[285] All considered, Galdós showed an enlightened interest in, and sympathy for, the Jews. His attitude reveals itself again in his picture of Daniel Morton.

Daniel is a Sephardic Jew, born in Hamburg, a resident of Altona and of London, who has lived three and a half years in Córdoba and Seville.[286] He is a handsome, blue-eyed[287] young man whose beautiful profile closely resembles that of Christ.[288] His education is broad; his philosophical outlook is enlightened;[289] his only flaw is racial intolerance.[290] He cannot forget the persecution the Hebrews have suffered these many centuries and rallies to his religion as a substitute for the lost Jewish nationalism. Even as a youth he brooded over the future of his people until he was almost driven mad with the tension.[291]

Later, after his shipwreck in Ficóbriga, he is swept away by an irresistible passion for Gloria, the Spanish Catholic girl. The price of Gloria's hand, that is, the sacrifice of his religion, or more accurately, of his family affections, racial traditions, and pride in the superiority of his group – this price is at first too great

[282] *Obras completas*, Aguilar, VI, 1659.
[283] *Ibid.*, VI, 1739.
[284] *Ibid.*; see "Censo de personajes" at end of Vols. III and VI.
[285] *Ibid.*, III, 144 (*O'Donnell*, Chap. IX).
[286] *Gloria*, p. 531 (I, 19).
[287] *Ibid.*
[288] *Ibid.*, pp. 526 (I, 16), 575 (I, 37), and 644 (II, 22).
[289] *Ibid.*, pp. 532 (I, 20) and 542 (I, 23).
[290] *Ibid.*, pp. 614 (II, 11) and 618 (II, 12).
[291] *Ibid.*, p. 658 (II, 28).

for Daniel to pay. But when he finds that Gloria has borne him a child, he is willing to submit to a feigned conversion, from which his mother's fanatic intervention preserves him. Yet as Gloria dies, he does simulate a conversion to ease her final moments. Three years later he dies insane, after two years of madly seeking the new, all-embracing religion of the future.

The treatment of Daniel Morton implies considerable literary influence, some of general tendencies, some of particular works. When all is said and done, we shall find that Daniel, like other elements of the novel, is a composite of the most diverse suggestions – the romantic hero, Don Quijote, Benito Spinoza, Heinrich Heine, the Wandering Jew, Jesus, and Don Ignacio Bauer. Here again we shall see that Galdós was preparing to create this character by some of his anticipatory reading.

Romanticism was by no means dead in the Spanish novel of the 1870s, even in the early novels of Galdós himself. There are numerous traces of it, especially in its later humanitarian form represented by Eugène Sue and Hugo's *Les Misérables*. Of course Galdós thought of himself as a realist,[292] but he did not learn the meaning of realism at the beginning; in fact, throughout his life his concept of realism undergoes several changes which bring with them his various artistic modes. And it was hard for Galdós to think of a Jew without coloring his vision with romanticism.

Specifically, Daniel arrives in Ficóbriga, after Gloria has felt a powerful presentiment of his coming,[293] amid the turbulence of the shipwreck; his first return is also accompanied by a storm.[294] He is driven to return by an irresistible, fatal force.[295] He is long a man of mystery, his true origin and background being unknown to the Spaniards. When they know all about him, he is then an outcast from society and is driven constantly onward like Eugenie Sue's Wandering Jew.[296] He is overcome with a fatal love

[292] Berkowitz, *Pérez Galdós,* p. 93.
[293] *Gloria,* p. 520 (I, 14).
[294] *Ibid.*, p. 574 (I, 36).
[295] *Ibid.*, p. 576 (I, 37).
[296] See this description of Daniel: "Por fin, cuando la noche avanzó más, por los cerros lejanos, tierra adentro, se veía un jinete que marchaba despacio, inclinada la cabeza sobre el pecho. Su figura negra no era favorable

for Gloria,[297] who, by the way, is no *femme fatale*. He has a presentiment of misfortune from the beginning of their love.[298] Nevertheless, his soul is fatally and mysteriously chained to hers.[299] He can exclaim, "Mi pasión ha sido más fuerte que yo . . ." and, "He sido juguete de misteriosas fuerzas."[300] Without doubt he is, in part, a romantic hero. Almost all the romanticism in the novel centers in his figure.[301]

An interesting parallel can be made between Daniel Morton and Daniel Deronda in George Eliot's novel. The English novelist, who was just as much a realist as Galdós, could not refrain from giving many romantic tints to the story of her Jewish hero. Deronda is brought up in ignorance of his origin and does not even know he is a Jew until he meets his long-lost mother. But even before the dramatic revelation of his racial origin the *cri du sang* begins to work, inciting his interest in the Jews. A number of melodramatic coincidences result – events hardly to be classed as realistic. Deronda rescues a young woman from drowning. She is the Jewess, Mirah, who eventually becomes his wife. While searching for her brother, Ezra Cohen, he finds him, without recognizing him as such, under the name of Mordecai. A spiritual affinity draws him to this new friend and under his direction he devotes his life to the study of Hebrew and Judaism. All this takes place before Daniel Deronda knows himself to be a Jew.

a la armonía del risueño paisaje: diríase que después que él pasaba, todo volvía a estar alegre," *ibid.*, p. 557 (I, 28); see also Part II, Chap. 9, "El Maldito," in which Daniel can find no one who will offer him friendship or shelter in Ficóbriga. With this we should compare the first description of the Wandering Jew in Sue's work. Ahasverus walks slowly along a wild mountainside, overlooking a fertile and usually peaceful and happy valley. But his presence brings on desolation and death. He walks with his head sunk on his breast, as the sun sets and night comes on. He meditates on his punishment, never to repose or to find friendly welcome, always to be driven on, a cursed man. See *Le Juif Errant*, Part II, Chap. 3, end.

[297] *Gloria*, p. 615 (II, 11): "Mi insensato y desvariado amor . . ." and p. 658 (II, 28): ". . . el fatal encadenamiento de su alma con la mía."

[298] *Ibid.*, p. 550 (I, 26).

[299] *Ibid.*, p. 664 (II, 29): "Entre su pensamiento y el mío, como entre nuestros corazones, existe una cadena misteriosa."

[300] *Ibid.*, p. 578 (I, 37).

[301] Some elements of romanticism surround Gloria during and just before her death scene.

Although *Daniel Deronda* (published February 1 to June 3, 1876) precedes *Gloria* (December 1876) by only a short time, I cannot find the slightest trace of influence of the English novel upon the Spanish one. The interest in the comparison is merely that neither one of the two realistic novelists could conceive a Jew without the trappings of romanticism.

Because Daniel Morton seeks an ideal and almost impossible solution – the brotherhood of all men through the religion of the future – Galdós has equated him to Don Quijote in the second part of *Gloria*. We know from Galdós' other novels that even a hint of idealism always brings the author back to Cervantes as a model.[302] In this case, when our hero comes back to Ficóbriga for the second time, bringing his servant Sansón with him, the parallelism between the master and man and the *hidalgo* and Sancho Panza becomes immediately apparent.

The "descomunal contienda" between the Ficobrigans and Sansón is treated humorously; Sansón, like Sancho, suffers a broken head.[303] Even the language takes on an archaic, Quixotic flavor.[304] The squire Sansón is quite as talkative as his prototype. He makes the same abundant use of proverbs as Sancho, although his sayings are all of Biblical origin.[305] But these accessory details are purely ornamental: the important factor in regard to the structure of the whole novel is the idealism of Daniel. At an earlier date, his youthful meditations on the destiny and history of his race so inflamed his mind that he almost lost his senses. He explains, "Mi juventud ha sido un delirio doloroso, un sueño en que se han confundido los intentos más atrevidos con las ideas

[302] J. Chalmers Herman ("*Don Quijote* and the Novels of Pérez Galdós," unpublished Ph.D. thesis, University of Kansas) deals with the numerous Quixotic elements in the *Novelas Contemporáneas*. Antonio Obaid's "El *Quijote* en los *Episodios Nacionales* de Pérez Galdós" (unpublished Ph.D. thesis, University of Minnesota, 1953), treats the same elements in the *Episodios Nacionales*. He finds that forty-five out of the forty-six *Episodios* have parts influenced by the *Quijote*.

[303] *Gloria*, pp. 603–604 (II, 8).

[304] *Ibid.*, p. 622 (II, 14): ". . . si no exageran los autores que de esto han tratado . . ." etc.

[305] See p. 73 of this volume, n. 223.

más nobles. He soñado con la rehabilitación del judaísmo, con borrar la maldición horrible . . ." [306]

Later, the direction of his idealism changes somewhat as he seeks to incorporate Judaism along with the other religions into an all-embracing, overreligion. His mother makes clear the *quijotismo* of his position: ". . . siempre tuviste demasiado entusiasmo por la Escritura, y has pasado parte de tu vida comentándola . . . Ultimamente . . . te engolfaste de tal modo en la teología rabínica, que tuvimos que tapiar tu biblioteca, como la del gran caballero español. Vivías exaltado y melancólico . . . ¡Cuán cierto fué mi presagio de que tu mente se desquiciaba! . . . No puedo decir que no haya cierta grandeza en tus concepciones; pero lo que sí aseguro es que no hay en ellas sentido común." [307]

Along with Don Quijote and the romantic hero, a factor which we may call "the Rothschild type" worked toward the formation of Daniel Morton. Galdós was, of course, aware of the immense reputation of the Rothschilds, not merely as financial wizards, but also as patrons and collectors of art, munificent contributors to charity, and society hosts on a lavish scale.[308] In Madrid itself there were two families of Jewish financiers – the Weisweillers and the Bauers – who were agents of the Rothschilds and their imitators in every respect. Galdós mentions them by name in other novels [309] and unquestionably alludes to them in *Gloria* itself.[310]

These international Jewish financiers had nothing to fear from intolerance. Even the neo-Catholic banker Don Buenaventura Lantigua esteems their friendship. Above all, they were necessary to the functioning of the modern state. Of one such family it is

[306] *Gloria*, p. 615 (II, 11).
[307] *Ibid.*, p. 658 (II, 28).
[308] See E. C. Corti, *The Reign of the House of Rothschild*, New York, Cosmopolitan Book Corp., 1928.
[309] *Obras completas*, Aguilar, III, 144 (*O'Donnell*, Chap. IX) and III, 677 (*La de los tristes destinos*, Chap. X).
[310] *Gloria*, pp. 611 (II, 11) and 617 (II, 12). In the second passage he speaks of "el barón de W.," undoubtedly Daniel Weisweiller, who was made a baron in 1870.

said: "Subvencionaba ministros, compraba periódicos, y reunía en su mesa suntuosa a escritores famosos, políticos avanzados y prelados de la Iglesia Católica." [311]

Galdós created the Morton family in the image of the Rothschilds. Both Daniel's mother and father were Sephardim, the aristocrats of the Jews, although the father's line had been crossed with German and Dutch Israelites. The family possessed immense wealth, and consequently great power. Kings, ministers of finance, even the pope and his cardinals sought them out, entertained them lavishly, and bestowed titles and decorations upon them. They also were esteemed as collectors and patrons of the arts.[312] The treatment accorded to the Mortons in Galdós' fictitious world is exactly that given the Rothschilds in real life.

While Don Benito could know of the Rothschilds only by newspaper accounts, his acquaintance with "the Rothschild type" was based on living models, chief of whom was probably Don Ignacio Bauer. This is the financier whom Galdós called "el simpático y bondadoso don Ignacio," and whose literary friendships and luxurious dinners, well seasoned with lively conversation on literary, artistic, and learned subjects, were famous in his day. Among his friends, Don Ignacio numbered Valera, Aldana, Albareda, and Correa, of whom the last two were close friends and journalistic collaborators of Galdós. Like the Rothschilds, Don Ignacio was a patron of the arts, an urbane host, and constant, although often anonymous, contributor to charities. Government ministers, prelates of the church, and magnates of the aristocracy often sought his aid to prop their sagging finances.[313]

[311] R. Cansinos Assens, *Los judíos en Sefard,* Buenos Aires, Editorial Israel, 1950, p. 62.

[312] *Gloria,* p. 653 (II, 26).

[313] Eusebio Blasco, *Mis contemporáneos,* p. 59ff; in addition, I have at hand letters from the present head of the Bauer family, also named Don Ignacio, who kindly gave me biographical data about his grandfather. The latter was born in Budapest in 1827, left Hungary in 1848, and established himself as a partner of Don Daniel Weisweiller in Madrid in 1851. He died in 1895. His brother Bernardo had a most colorful career. After becoming a Jesuit he reached high places (e.g., confessor of the Empress Eugénie) but later, abandoning the church, he became a noted follower of horse racing.

Thus Don Ignacio Bauer and his family helped form the type to which Daniel Morton and his family belonged. But the resemblance between Daniel and Don Ignacio did not stop at these generalities. Bauer's physical traits conform to the description of our Jewish hero. The former is described as a handsome man, "el tipo israelita en todo su esplendor. Es como si dijéramos el Cristo repuesto de su campaña en este bajo mundo, y acabada en el cielo su convalescencia de la crucifixión. ¡Es Nuestro Señor . . . gordo!"[314] Daniel, too, is constantly described as resembling Jesus, especially the image of the crucified Saviour which was the property of the Lantigua family.

I do not mean, of course, that Don Ignacio was the unique physical model of Daniel Morton, only that his handsome, Christlike features contributed to the picture that Galdós presents us. There is the possibility that Daniel's portrait was based on some statue, as suggested in the novel itself, or on some painting of the Christ.[315] But the fact that Galdós shifts the exact nature of the statue of Christ to which he compares Daniel makes me believe he had no specific statuary model in mind.

We are first told that the hero's head resembles that of the Christ in a crystal urn within the Abadía.[316] This image must have been small, as shown by the urn; yet later Don Benito describes minutely the statue to which his creation is constantly compared as a life-sized figure mounted on a donkey.[317] At other times he momentarily compares Daniel's features with other images of the crucified Saviour which happen to be in the same room with the living Israelite.[318] This shifting of models shows pretty conclusively that Galdós had not decided beforehand to paint his hero in the likeness of some definite representation of

[314] *Ibid.*, p. 60.

[315] Compare with the fact that George Eliot took the likeness of Daniel Deronda from the Christ in Titian's "Tribute Money."

[316] *Gloria*, p. 526 (I, 16). There is, in fact, an agonizing Christ in a glass case in the church of Santillana, but his pain-racked face could hardly have been the model for the calm portrait of Daniel.

[317] *Ibid.*, pp. 590–591 (II, 4).

[318] *Ibid.*, pp. 575 (I, 37) and 644 (II, 22).

Christ. He merely wants to shock the neo-Catholics – as indeed those of the novel are shocked by Daniel's resemblance to the holy images [319] – with a statement of the Jewishness of Jesus.

Even Gloria, when she finally hears Daniel say he is a Jew, exclaims: ". . . ¿por qué no tuviste mala apariencia, como tienes mala religión? ¿Por qué no fueron horribles tus acciones, tus palabras y tu persona, como lo es tu creencia?" [320] She blurts out the typical Spanish reaction to the Jew, to which Galdós replies: "Your Saviour was a Jew."

The Jewish appearance of Jesus was stressed by the nineteenth-century philosophers who saw Jesus primarily as a man. Thus Renan pointed out that Jesus was born of Jewish stock and grew to manhood among Syrian peasants "whose appearance, education, and racial character he shared." [321] He believes that Christ had "une de ces ravissantes figures qui apparaissent quelquefois dans la race juive . . ." [322] Hartmann exclaims: "Jesus was emphatically a Jew. He lived and died in the circle of his time and of his nation, partaking in the superstition of the former, as well as having all the national faith of the latter in prophecies . . . Jesus, I repeat, was a Jew, and nothing but a Jew." [323] These and many other philosophers were shocking the religious conservatives of their times.

Although a statue of Jesus was not the immediate source of the description of Daniel, Galdós frequently used pictorial models for his characters. In one novel, *Fortunata y Jacinta*, Bringas looks like Thiers, la Caña like Cavour, and Mauricia *la dura* like Napoleon, all of which famous persons Galdós could have known only by pictures. Estupiñá looks like Rossini, whose bust adorned music-lover Galdós' study. In short, Galdós often used pictorial models. The model for Daniel Morton, if there were one, would

[319] *Ibid.*, pp. 549 (I, 25) and 592 (II, 5).

[320] *Ibid.*, p. 576 (I, 37).

[321] Mme James Darmesteter, *The Life of Ernest Renan,* London, 1898, p. 161.

[322] Renan, *Vie de Jésus*, p. 84.

[323] Edward von Hartmann, *The Religion of the Future,* transl. by Ernest Dare, London, 1886, p. 50. The same idea was expressed in the Cortes of 1869: see M. Pelayo, *Heterodoxos*, ed. Artigas, VII, 430.

have to be the representation of a Jew whose features greatly resembled those of Jesus.[324]

The portrait of Heinrich Heine which appeared in the French translation of his *Reisebilder* (1858) has exactly these qualities. Heine himself, speaking of a slightly different version of the same portrait which had already appeared in the *Revue des deux mondes*, says: ". . . l'on me représente émacié et penchant la tête comme un Christ de Moralès . . ."[325] Théophile Gautier describes him from life in the same vein: ". . . la maladie l'avait atténué, émacié, disséqué comme à plaisir; et dans la statue du dieu grec taillait avec la patience minutieuse d'un artiste du moyen âge un Christ décharné jusqu'au squelette, où les nerfs, les tendons, les veines apparaissaient en saillie."[326] Certainly the portrait does not stress the emaciated appearance of the poet nearly as much as the verbal descriptions: in it appears a beautiful, pathetic, calmly suffering, Christlike countenance. It corresponds perfectly to the description of Daniel Morton just after his shipwreck.

Gloria first notices ". . . un rostro lívido y dolorido . . . entreabierta la boca, cerrados los ojos, ligeramente fruncido el ceño . . . El perfil de aquella cara era perfecto, la frente hermosísima, entre obscuros cabellos desordenados. De las cejas rectas, ligeramente arqueadas hacia la sien, partía la nariz aguileña, fina, intachable, como cortada por diestro cincel. Bigote castaño y barba del mismo color, un poco puntiaguda y ligeramente bifur-

[324] Without leaving *Gloria* we find evidence of Galdós' tendency to think in pictures. When the Holy Week procession is broken up by Daniel's arrival, Don Benito says: "El cuadro de Goya *La Procesión dispersada por la lluvia* puede dar idea de tal escena" (*Gloria*, p. 604; II, 8). See also the description of Caifás and Gloria in the sacristy, on which Galdós comments: "No era posible mayor semejanza con los cuadros en que el arte ha puesto una figura mundana orando de rodillas al pie de la Virgen María" (*ibid.*, p. 522; I, 15).

[325] *Reisebilder – Tableaux de voyage*, p. ii. The portrait appeared in the *Revue des deux mondes* in April 1852. The engraving was slightly changed for publication in the *Reisebilder*, the most significant change being the expression of the mouth. In the *Revue* Heine wears a faint, ironical, mocking smile; in the *Reisebilder* the smile is gone and the feeling of resignation and pathos is heightened.

[326] *Reisebilder*, p. vi.

cada en su extremidad, remataban dignamente un rostro que era de los más acabados que pueden imaginarse. Gloria . . . hizo un paralelo rápido entre la cabeza que tenía delante y la del Señor . . ."[327] There are certain details in this description, especially the straight eyebrows slightly arched toward the temples, which are so peculiar to the portrait as to make me think that Galdós was copying it in his words. But we must look a little further before we jump to conclusions.

First let us look at Heine in Galdós' library. He had five works, all in French: *Reisebilder* (1863, a reprint of the edition containing the portrait and the introduction by Théophile Gautier), *Poèmes et Légendes* (1861), *De l'Allemagne* (1866), *Lutèce* (1866), and *De la France* (1867). The dates of these editions, the marking of the first two works, and the knowledge of Heine shown in one of Galdós' youthful articles[328] are indications of the Spaniard's early interest in and acquaintance with the German.

Galdós would, of course, have known of Heine's Jewish origin. He could not help recalling the many allusions to the Jews in Heine's prose. He would furthermore be aware of the numerous references to Hamburg, especially in *Schnabelewopski* (included in the *Reisebilder*), which is an imaginary autobiography of Heine. From Heine, Galdós would realize that Hamburg was an industrial and banking center and that its Jews, including Heine's Uncle Solomon, were active in its banks and stock exchange. Hamburg appears so commonly in Heine's works that Matthew Arnold erroneously states that Heine was a native of that city.[329]

Although Heine was not born there, Daniel Morton was. But he now resides in Altona, a suburb of Hamburg.[330] This town is so completely unknown to Galdós' Spanish characters and readers that he takes pains to explain where it is. How would Galdós

[327] *Gloria,* pp. 525–526 (I, 16).

[328] *Obras completas*, Aguilar, VI, 1633–1634. Let us not forget that Heine and, more specifically, his *Reisebilder* are named by Galdós in an autobiographical passage which reflects Don Benito's own youthful reading. See p. 13.

[329] See "Heinrich Heine" in *Essays in Criticism*, New York: Macmillan, 1880.

[330] *Gloria,* p. 531 (I, 19).

know about it? Why didn't he choose one of the more famous settlements of the Sephardim—Amsterdam or London[331]—as the place of origin of his hero?

As to the first question, he probably remembered Altona from his readings of Heine.[332] In one passage Heine speaks of the Rabbi of Altona.[333] If Galdós consulted his encyclopedia, he found that Altona had an important colony of Sephardim and a famous old Jewish burial ground. As to the second question, I suggest that Daniel came from Altona and Hamburg rather than Amsterdam or London merely because Heine was associated with them in Don Benito's mind and that he was thinking about Heine as he wrote this part of *Gloria.*

Now the mention of Altona occurs only a few pages after the description of Daniel which I thought was largely based on the portrait of Heine. It shows that Galdós was thinking of Heine at this point in the book; nowhere else in the novel does the name Altona recur. In later chapters Daniel and his family are always said to reside in London, although Hamburg is sometimes mentioned as the place of Daniel's birth. Perhaps also the blue eyes of our hero—popularly thought to be unusual in a Jew—are borrowed from Heine. Galdós could know of their color from Gautier's introduction to the *Reisebilder.*[334] Yet it is strange that the Spanish novelist did not give Daniel Heine's blond hair also.[335]

A final point worthy of mention is that Galdós does not describe Daniel's body, concentrating all the beauties of his

[331] When Galdós himself names the principal cities in which the dispersed Sephardim are found he mentions "Constantinopla, Salónica, Jerusalén, Venecia, Roma, el Cairo" (*ibid.*, p. 653; II, 26), but says nothing of the centers in western Europe.

[332] In *Schnabelewopski,* Chap. III, Altona is said to be one of the sights of Hamburg; it appears again in Chap. IV.

[333] *De l'Allemagne,* Part I, Book 2.

[334] *Reisebilder,* p. iii. Later, in the second part (*Gloria,* p. 590; II, 4), the Christ of the Lantiguas, which is supposed to resemble Daniel very much, has black eyes.

[335] Galdós was apparently not very sensitive to color. He often drew black and white sketches of his characters to help him keep their features in mind. Working from the portrait of Heine, where the hair is certainly not light in tone, he may have forgotten or deliberately ignored Gautier's

physical make-up in his face. This would point again to the portrait of Heine, whose body was at that time wasted almost to nothing, and is not prominent in the portrait. Even the description of the Christ of the Lantiguas concentrates all attention on the head, and the author tells us that the body was the work of the carpenter rather than the sculptor.[336]

If externally Daniel Morton conforms to "the Rothschild type" and more specifically to Ignacio Bauer and Heinrich Heine, his inner make-up differs considerably from these models. The tolerance and compromising spirit which they possessed toward all social problems existed only with reference to religion with him. His Quixotic desire to bring about a solution to all religious conflict came into opposition with a great racial fanaticism, which was the strongest force in his character. The externalization of this conflict – that is, the attempt to find a solution by which Daniel can marry Gloria without giving up his Judaism – provides the action for the second part of the novel. For Gloria, once she knows that Daniel is a Jew, never seriously considers marrying him without his previous conversion to Christianity.

The conflict in Daniel's soul becomes the leading thread of the second part of *Gloria*. This conflict was not natural to "the Rothschild type" or to Heine. Did Galdós invent it out of nothing? To present it to us he would have to be aware of the intense attachment of the Jew to family tradition, his feeling that religion replaced the lost fatherland, that the indignities and sufferings of exile and torture found a compensation in the dignity and elevation his religion instilled in him. His pride of race and feeling of superiority were other factors, all of which would work together to maintain the Jew firm in his faith, but on a sociological more than a truly religious basis.[337]

Galdós did know of this "fanaticism of race" and depicted

verbal description, which mentions the blond hair. William H. Shoemaker, "Galdós' Literary Creativity: D. José Ido del Sagrario" in *Hispanic Review*, XIX (1951), 212, has some interesting observations on this point. Galdós described Ido's hair now as red, now as black.

[336] *Gloria*, p. 591 (II, 4).

[337] *Ibid.*, p. 655 (II, 27): "Madre, me has hablado de honor, de vergüenza, de familia; en fin, me has dado razones sociales, no religiosas."

it well.[338] But the Jews he knew in Madrid were not the kind to feel this sentiment strongly. He may have heard something of it orally or he may have read something about it in factual works such as histories of the Jews. It is unlikely that the knowledge came from casual references, for the average Christian, especially if he is Spanish, is so convinced of the inferiority of the Jews that their belief in their own superiority never comes to his attention.

The chief source of Galdós' awareness of Jewish fanaticism was probably Auerbach's novelized version of Spinoza's life, which appeared under a Spanish title *Benito Espinosa* in 1876, after having run serially in the *Revista Europea* from December 26, 1875, to February 27, 1876. Its translator, U. Gonzáles Serrano, was a youthful *krausista* professor (Salmerón's assistant) and an active member of the Ateneo. A reviewer in *Madrid literario* (November 19, 1876) said, "Benito Espinosa debía luchar contra la [intolerancia] de su familia, bien así como su familia hubo de luchar contra nuestra intolerancia." Here we have the two forces, Jewish fanaticism and Spanish fanaticism, which are to oppose each other in *Gloria*. The second is only vaguely felt in the yearning of the Sephardim to return to Spain, but the first is analyzed in detail.

Auerbach, himself of Jewish origin, paints the Hebrews with much local color and knowledge of customs and rituals. He also knows well the philosophical currents of the Germany of his time, in which Spinoza's influence was of prime importance. He shows how Spinoza begins to doubt Judaism, how he becomes convinced that an all-embracing, tolerant cult must take its place: "Una voz más fuerte y penetrante que la de la sinagoga obligaba a Baruch a bendecir la ley manifiesta, aunque no escrita, que proclama la caridad universal y la renuncia a todo egoismo de secta o creencia. Aceptaba la afirmación de Maimonides, de que los piadosos de todas las religiones logran la felicidad eterna. Baruch dejó de ser hijo de Israel para ser hijo de la humanidad."[339]

[338] *Ibid.*, pp. 614–615 (II, 11), 618 (II, 12), 653 (II, 26), and 672 (II, 32).
[339] *Benito Espinosa*, p. 37.

This passage and a number of similar ones explain why a *krausista* saw fit to translate this particular work into Spanish. Quibbling over dogma is decried,[340] reason is exalted,[341] and conscience is proclaimed the supreme judge.[342] Religion is an internal force and becomes fanatic only when some people try to make it "la palabra de orden para toda la sociedad."[343] The translation of Auerbach must be reckoned as another attempt at *krausista* propaganda, like Villarminio's and Azcárate's works.

Baruch's ideas soon alienate his family and his Jewish friends. Ultimately the synagogue solemnly excommunicates and anathematizes him,[344] his sisters weep for him as if he were dead,[345] and a former companion even tries to assassinate him. Jewish fanaticism is a powerful force; its most obvious incarnation is in Baruch's sister Miriam, who had been his closest boyhood companion. She replaces to some extent Baruch's dead mother. She tries to draw him back to orthodoxy by her fervent love, alternating its protestations with threats of absolute separation if he persists in his beliefs.[346]

Here we see the germ of Esther Spinoza (note the surname), Daniel's mother. Both women use the same arguments, dwelling on the shame which will fall on the family and stressing the exemplariness of the family's conduct throughout the centuries of exile. The abandoning of this tradition, just when each hero seems destined to carry the family name to new heights of glory, must have the same result in each case. The family will mourn its black sheep as dead, not as an apostate. This typically Jewish ritual – which it is doubtful that Galdós would have known without having read Auerbach – is brought into great prominence.

Another notable parallel between *Benito Espinosa* and *Gloria*

[340] *Ibid.*, p. 38.
[341] *Ibid.*, pp. 52 and 61.
[342] *Ibid.*, p. 104.
[343] *Ibid.*, p. 176; compare with the attitude of Don Juan de Lantigua shown above, p. 32.
[344] *Ibid.*, p. 157.
[345] *Ibid.*, p. 160.
[346] *Ibid.*, p. 142.

Ignacio Bauer, one of the possible models for Daniel Morton (see page 94).

Heinrich Heine, another of the possible models for Daniel Morton (see page 97).

is the love affair between a Jewish youth and a Catholic girl. At the outset we should note that Auerbach cannot develop the theme dramatically in his book, as his better informed readers would know that Spinoza never married and lived an unusually calm, extraworldly life. Thus Olympia van den Ende, the Catholic daughter of one of Spinoza's teachers, is resisted by the philosopher,[347] who foresees religious controversy and who cannot commit the perjury of adopting a religion in which he does not believe.[348] Passion brings the lovers as far as a kiss,[349] but Spinoza's yearning for Olympia's companionship, especially after his excommunication, is thwarted by the appearance of a rival.[350] The girl, weary of the philosopher's resistance, accepts and marries another.[351] There is considerable talk about whether a lover should sacrifice his religion for his love,[352] and Spinoza even dreams that he is converted in order to marry Olympia.[353]

This love affair was fictitious, although based on a tradition buried in an obscure Latin source.[354] Thus if Galdós knew it at all, he must have read about it in Auerbach. But can we prove that he actually did read this book?

Our only arguments are indirect ones. First, he was a friend of the translator, who had reviewed favorably his *Doña Perfecta*,[355] who shared his liberal ideas, and who also frequented the Ateneo.[356] A number of other works of González Serrano are in Galdós' library. Then, when he thought of Jews, his thoughts would naturally turn to notable examples of the race, as we have seen in the case of Heinrich Heine. As the Morton

[347] *Ibid.*, pp. 106–110.
[348] *Ibid.*, p. 110.
[349] *Ibid.*, p. 113.
[350] *Ibid.*, p. 133.
[351] *Ibid.*, pp. 162 and 168.
[352] *Ibid.*, p. 166.
[353] *Ibid.*, pp. 114–115.
[354] See James Martineau, *A Study of Spinoza*, London, 1882, pp. 24–25.
[355] The review is reprinted in his *Ensayos de crítica y filosofía*, Madrid, 1881, p. 203ff.
[356] Galdós describes him in the Ateneo during the Revolution of 1868, calling him a "filósofo precoz" (*Obras completas*, Aguilar, III, 579; *Prim*, Chap. XIII).

family is of Spanish origin, he certainly would think of the most distinguished of all Spanish Jews, Baruch Spinoza. That he did so is evident from the surname Spinoza given to Daniel's mother. His interest in Heine, too, would lead him back to Spinoza, for the German poet narrates the Jewish philosopher's life and emphasizes his great significance for modern liberal thought.[357] All this shows that Galdós would have read the Auerbach novel with interest, if he knew of it, and that, given his friendship with the translator, he was probably aware of its existence.

If *Gloria* ended with the first part we should have practically nothing on Jewish fanaticism. Galdós felt like dropping the subject there but was persuaded to squeeze the subject dry by an unnamed critic,[358] who could well be González Serrano himself. In the latter's review of *Doña Perfecta* the only fault he finds with the book is precisely that it ends too abruptly. He will not end his review, he states, ". . . sin dolernos de que el autor de *Doña Perfecta* haya precipitado de un modo incomprensible el desenlace de su obra."

Stipulating what a good "obra literaria" should be, he generalizes his criticism as follows: ". . . preciso es que en ella [i.e., la obra] no falten tampoco la acción y la vida y el completo desarrolo de esta acción y de esta vida; que sólo de esta suerte obrando y viviendo, hasta el fin y hasta sus últimas consecuencias, puede lograr el artista, según prescribía constantemente Goethe, la identificación de lo real con lo ideal, que es la primera y superior condición de toda obra bella."[359]

We must envisage the possibility that Galdós, while still planning or writing Part One of *Gloria*, discussed it with González Serrano, and that the latter, remembering *Doña Perfecta* (written only a few months before) urged Galdós to exhaust the ultimate consequences of this new subject. If they got this far they undoubtedly also talked of the Jewish theme, *Benito Espi-*

[357] *De l'Allemagne*, Part I, Book 2.

[358] See page 18 of this volume, first paragraph.

[359] U. González Serrano, *Ensayos de crítica y de filosofía*, pp. 205–206.

nosa, and Jewish fanaticism. Note that the influence of Auerbach's book appears only in the second part of *Gloria*, that Jewish fanaticism is a theme confined entirely to the second part, and finally that the treatment of *Jewish* fanaticism does "apurar el tema" since the first part was devoted primarily to *Christian* intolerance. All these details hint that González Serrano was the critic who suggested that *Gloria* be extended.[360]

Another significant point is one of Galdós' inconsistencies, one of the unskillfully welded joints in his raw material. He has made the Morton family in the pattern of the international financiers. Daniel himself is described as "una persona bien nacida, de trato muy afable, de carácter noble y recto, delicadísima, y adornada con instrucción tan vasta que en casa de Lantigua todos estaban atónitos."[361] This is in keeping with the broad knowledge of current philosophical and religious discussion which he shows,[362] but it is not in accord with the rather narrow Talmudic studies to which Daniel is supposed to have devoted his youth[363] and the racial intolerance which he is said to feel.[364]

In other words, Daniel is first the Rothschild type and then the unassimilated Jew, a patent contradiction which I think comes from the imperfect welding of two models. The second of these in my opinion is the youthful Baruch Spinoza, his family, and his boyhood companions, as portrayed by Auerbach.

[360] That the second part was indeed an afterthought is suggested by internal evidence. Don Buenaventura and Doña Serafinita, who figure so largely in the second part, are mentioned only once in Part One, where Galdós says: "No entrando, por ahora, en nuestros fines estos dos últimos, los dejamos a un lado . . ." (Chap. 4). Later, on reintroducing them in Chapter 1, Part Two, he says: "En el capítulo IV de la primera parte se hizo rápida mención de estas dos estimables personas; más no era entonces ocasión de hablar mucho de ellos; ahora, sí." It seems almost certain that the first allusion to these two characters was added either in the manuscript or the proofs; otherwise they would have been woven more skillfully and artistically into the tale. My attempts to locate the manuscript and proofs of *Gloria* have been fruitless, so my opinion cannot be verified.

[361] *Gloria*, p. 532 (I, 20).

[362] *Ibid.*, p. 542 (I, 23).

[363] *Ibid.*, p. 658 (II, 28).

[364] *Ibid.*, p. 638 (II, 20): ". . . al considerar la idea cristiana, nuestro verdugo y nuestro cadalso, soy fanático y brutal como los inquisidores católicos . . ." Daniel makes several other such declarations.

Both young men's brilliant Talmudic studies lead their families to the highest hopes for their future careers, which in both cases are deceived by a growing liberalism of thought. In Daniel's case racial intolerance lives on despite religious tolerance.

In sum, Galdós probably knew González Serrano's translation and took from it Jewish fanaticism in general and the attitude of Esther Spinoza in particular. He got from it knowledge of certain Jewish rituals, such as considering the apostate as already dead. He also got some more narrowly Jewish characteristics for Daniel Morton, who could otherwise have developed into the Jewish freethinker—a type represented in real life by Heine, despite his conversion to Christianity. Then Galdós' novel would have conformed to the usual pattern of the nineteenth-century religious novel showing the freethinker in love with a Catholic girl.

Daniel Morton is the most composite of all the creations of *Gloria*. Each factor that goes into Daniel's make-up accounts only for a small part of his physical, mental, or moral traits. It is far more difficult to disengage the component factors here than in the cases we have already examined; for, as we saw in studying Galdós' topography, one model may be uppermost in the author's mind for a chapter or two and then give way to another. From his conscious and subconscious assimilation of many elements we can conclude that Galdós' search for material was wider and more exhaustive in this instance than in the case of his other characters.

MORE ABOUT CHARACTERS

Besides observing the complicated and at times even contradictory elements which went into the formation of Daniel Morton, we have seen that Gloria combines suggestions from Juanita Lund and Sibylle, that Don Angel and Silvestre Romero owe much to l'abbé Renaud, that Romero also derives from Prior Aymer, that Caifás and Rafael del Horro have their counterparts in Feuillet's novel, that Juan de Lantigua embodies the spirit of Pereda or Menéndez Pelayo combined with suggestions from Beaumanoir and Biblical prophets, that Sansón is a squire of the Sancho Panza type, and that Esther Spinoza has much in common with Miriam Spinoza of Auerbach's novel.

However, any such simple statement does not allow for the complexity of the characters. For example, the politicians Silvestre Romero and Rafael del Horro also owe something to the Biblical suggestion of the banquet to triumph over their enemies, and something to Galdós' acquaintance with living neo-Catholics and political leaders. Caifás surely derives some of his traits from the conventional Spanish notion that a sacristan is a good-for-nothing, usually a drunkard. Again direct observation must have supplied Galdós with details.

The town gossips (Teresita la monja, Isidorita la del Rebenque, and la Gobernadora de las armas) as well as Juan Amarillo, the mayor and usurer of Ficóbriga, are *costumbrista* types. Galdós, in describing them, may be drawing on direct observation, but his point of view is provided by Pereda. This seems evident from the passage in which he pictures the various peasant types marching in the religious procession, types which he says are "trasladados por Pereda con arte maravilloso al museo de sus célebres libros montañeses." [365]

Another indication of the Peredean origin of these characters is the title of the chapter, "Realismo," in which they are first seen in action.[366] Pereda was to Galdós above all a realist.[367] Galdós felt himself out of his element when dealing with *costumbrismo*. These characters, not essential to the organization of *Gloria*, are brought in for local color, but this color *a la Pereda* does not harmonize well with the over-all tone of the novel. The different emotional point of view from which they are conceived is the proof that they are not copied directly from life.[368]

[365] *Gloria*, p. 602 (II, 8).

[366] Part II, Chap. 5.

[367] See the review of *Tipos y paisajes* in *El Debate*, Jan. 26, 1872; also *Obras completas*, VI, 1487.

[368] Pierre Audiat (*La biographie de l'oeuvre littéraire*, p. 140) asserts that a diversity of emotional impressions felt by the reader is the sign of varied sources of inspiration on the part of the author.

There are still two important secondary characters to be discussed further – Don Buenaventura and Doña Serafinita. We have seen that they are two varieties of the neo-Catholic species. The first is the hypocrite, who is really a rationalist [369] but who clings to the outward forms because of social pressure. Thus for him the all-important thing is to save appearances, which he hopes to do by marrying Gloria to Daniel after a feigned conversion.[370] To him a compromise is the highest solution to all human problems.[371]

I find it impossible to put my finger on the specific individual or individuals who suggested Don Buenaventura to Galdós. Yet the type did exist. In the Ateneo, Galdós saw constantly José Moreno Nieto, for a long while the librarian and later the president of that institution as well as rector of the university after the expulsion of the *krausistas*. He is constantly described as a great antagonist of materialism, *krausismo*, and positivism, but one whose stanch Catholicism is often tainted with doubt.[372] In fact his election to the presidency of the Ateneo was due to his compromise position between Catholicism and rationalism.[373]

Galdós himself noted the same tendency in a youthful essay. Speaking of Moreno Nieto's eloquence he says: "Es la palabra del magnífico libre pensador moderno, animada y fortalecida con un destello del sublime espíritu de Santa Teresa." [374] Moreno Nieto's rationalism, hidden under a cloak of traditionalistic Catholicism, and his desire to make compromises between the two opposed forces make him a perfect living model for Don Buenaventura.

The type was not rare, which causes me to hesitate in ascribing a specific model to the Galdosian creation. In the political and journalistic fields the head of the Carlist party was Cándido

[369] *Gloria*, p. 613 (II, 11).
[370] *Ibid.*, p. 618 (II, 12).
[371] *Ibid.*, p. 617 (II, 12).
[372] A. Linares Rivas in *Revista de España*, 64 (1878), 91–103; Revilla in *Revista contemporánea*, I (1875), 128.
[373] Revilla, *op. cit.*, I, 387.
[374] "Galería de figuras de cera," in *Correo de España*, Feb. 13, 1871.

Nocedal. A man opposed to parliamentary government, he nonetheless advised Don Carlos (March 1871) not to begin another civil war, maintaining that through parliamentary procedures he could bring about the fall of liberalism and the triumph of the reactionaries. In much the same way Nocedal distrusted but used skillfully the power of the press. As Ministro de Gobernación (1857) he imposed rigid censorship rules on the press, but from his own paper, *La Constancia*, and from *El Siglo Futuro*, directed by his son, he kept up a vigorous and unrelenting attack on liberalism.

Young Galdós frequently combats the assertions of these newspapers in his journalistic works. Many times he derides Nocedal himself as the leader of the Carlists.[375] Yet it is obvious that Nocedal, like Don Buenaventura, had become infected with the germs of the malady he sought to eradicate. He used the congress and the press; he strove for a compromise. In short, Galdós must have gotten suggestions for his rationalistic reactionary from men like Moreno Nieto and Nocedal, but since there were a good many persons of this type, we cannot localize the influence.

The second variety of the neo-Catholic, Doña Serafinita, is above all the puritan. Her lack of human feeling leads Galdós to dub her with the nickname "the Mephistopheles of Heaven."[376] Although she certainly resembles Beaumanoir in *Ivanhoe*, the literary character who most recalls Doña Serafinita is Daya in Lessing's *Nathan the Wise*. Daya is the Christian nurse and governess of the heroine, Recha, who has been brought up in tolerant Deism by the Jew Nathan. Daya feels that Recha will surely be condemned to hell and that any effort made to bring her to Christianity, no matter how devious that effort may be, is right. Thus Recha can call her "my own good wicked Daya . . . at once so good and bad"[377] and say that she

[375] To cite but a few examples: *La Nación*, 1868, numbers of Jan. 12, Jan. 19, Jan. 26, and Apr. 5.

[376] *Gloria*, p. 664 (II, 29).

[377] G. E. Lessing, *Nathan the Wise*, transl. by P. Maxwell, New York, 1923, p. 345.

> Is one of those good simple Christian souls
> Who from sheer love must torture those they love;
> One of those kindly fanatics who think
> *They* only know the strait and narrow way,
> The one true way to God.[378]

This comparison is interesting but by no means a proof. In the first place, Galdós' library as now preserved contains nothing by Lessing. Against this it could be argued that if Galdós was seeking books of Jewish interest—as well as those which championed tolerance—he could well have been drawn to *Nathan the Wise*, one of the greatest of all such works. Furthermore in reading Heine's *De l'Allemagne* he would find high praise of Lessing, "the third liberator" of Germany, of his *Nathan the Wise*, and of Lessing's Jewish friend Moses Mendelssohn. When Galdós decided to write about a Jew and began to seek out Jewish source material, Heine's praise may have led him to Lessing.

In spite of this possibility, Galdós had so many living *beatas* to draw from that the literary model seems unnecessary. His own mother exhibited a puritanical sternness which is probably reflected in Doña Perfecta and the numerous other women of the same cast scattered throughout his works.[379]

Perhaps we can deduce a certain generalization or "law" of the creative process from this review of the characters of *Gloria*. First, those characters which most accurately reflect the dominant emotion of the novel have the least literary origin. In *Gloria*, Galdós is dominated by his usual hatred of fanaticism, indeed, but there is also the modifying factor of his friendship with the well-bred people of Santander, who have only a germ of what he calls intolerance. The dominant emotion was evoked by them; hence, naturally enough, in drawing characters to represent their spirit, Galdós did not have to go to literary models.

But as we look over the gallery of neo-Catholic types, we discover that the farther we remove ourselves from this center,

[378] *Ibid.*, pp. 345–346.
[379] Berkowitz, *Pérez Galdós*, p. 19.

the more literary models come into play. Thus the most perfect reflection of Pereda and Menéndez Pelayo is Don Juan de Lantigua, who shows few traces of literary prototypes. When we reach Don Angel, Silvestre Romero, and Rafael del Horro, we have characters formed under literary influences and, by the same token, characters who do not reflect so completely the spirit of people Galdós knew. If this "law" holds, then Don Buenaventura and Doña Serafinita, based, in my estimation, mainly on living models (although not types which Galdós necessarily associated with the north coast), must also reveal the dominating emotion of the author, specifically his opposition to hyprocrisy and puritanism.

But why is Daniel not a prime example of the dominant emotion of his creator? If he were indeed so, his composite literary origins invalidate our "law." But Daniel was not primarily a living person or persons who produced an emotion in Galdós which he later reproduced in the Daniel of the novel. Rather he is a *created* character, created probably with considerable difficulty to be an embodiment of an emotion derived from another source. Daniel has so complex an origin because Galdós had relatively little firsthand knowledge of the Jews. Hence his reading on Jewish subjects to prepare himself for *Gloria.*

THE CREATIVE PROCESS

We can now return to the statements made at the beginning of this chapter. Galdós as a creative writer did not create out of nothing. Stored in his mind was an immense amount of material – some derived from reading, some of it personal observations of men, buildings, and cities of la Montaña, some of it half-forgotten recollections of speeches in the Ateneo or Congreso, of conversations with friends, of newspaper accounts. For a number of years he felt the acute religious problem of Spain. This led him to read novels on religion, such as Feuillet's *Sibylle* and the novels of the *krausistas*. His sentiments were wholly favorable to the tolerant *krausista* point of view and equally opposed to neo-Catholic intolerance.

This attitude was strengthened by the repeal of religious tolerance and by the "separation" of the *krausista* professors from their chairs in the year before *Gloria* was written. Yet his friends in the north had shown him that neo-Catholics were not necessarily demons of fanaticism. Dominated by a hatred of intolerance, but striving to be as scrupulously fair as he could – such was the emotional attitude of Galdós before he conceived *Gloria.*

Somehow the idea of pitting Jewish intolerance against neo-Catholic intolerance entered his mind. Was it because he had visited Comillas and San Vicente de la Barquera the summer before? Both of these towns on the north coast had once had prosperous Jewish quarters, and Galdós, a great reader of guide books, probably knew about them. He must especially have known that Comillas (the birthplace of his friend Pereda's mother) had been granted by the Catholic monarchs to a "faithful subject for his zeal in driving the Jews from that part of the country."[380]

Perhaps the initial impetus came from some such tiny suggestion as Galdós could have found in one of Heine's letters, which was published in Spanish translation in 1875. The German poet says: ". . . se ha desarrollado también desde hace algún tiempo una grandísima tirantez entre los judíos bautizados y los no bautizados (todos los hamburgueses son, para mí, judíos; y los que, para distinguir de los circuncidados, llamo bautizados, son los que el vulgo llama cristianos). Con tal estado de cosas, se presume fácilmente que el amor cristiano no dejaría muy bien paradas las canciones de amor del judío."[381] Here we have the opposition between two fanaticisms which are, after all, essentially the same in quality. There is perhaps a hint that Galdós was thinking of Heine's phrase "judíos bautizados" when he calls one of his reactionary characters "el judío cristiano."[382] Then in the last sentence of the quotation from Heine there is the

[380] E. A. Peers, *Santander,* New York, Knopf, 1928, pp. 61 and 96.

[381] José del Perojo, *Ensayos sobre el movimiento intelectual en Alemania,* 1875, p. 50.

[382] *Gloria,* p. 580 (I, 38).

suggestion that a Jew's love would not find a cordial reception among reactionary Christians.

Of course a general current of liberal thought in favor of the Sephardim must be reckoned with, yet it seems likely that some more specific incident suggested the idea of a Jewish hero to Galdós. For this reason – whatever it might be – he began to read about the Jews.

The very word Jew would suggest to him Eugène Sue (*Le Juif errant*) and Heinrich Heine, both of whom he had surely read earlier. The name of Spinoza would also surely occur to him. In all probability Auerbach's novel, newly translated by his friend González Serrano, also reached his hands. He then looked into the Jewish poetry of the Bible, and was surprised to find the spirit of the neo-Catholic party of Spain foreshadowed in certain passages of the Psalms.

Things were about at this stage when Galdós, possibly just after leaving some discussion of the religious problem in the Ateneo, then located in the Calle de la Montera, passed through the Puerta del Sol on his way to the Café Universal. There the moment of crystallization took place. Out of the mass of material, consciously and subconsciously remembered, there flashed into place the elements necessary to make the first part of the novel. After two weeks of frenzied writing, it was down on paper.

THE CREATION OF *MARIANELA*

PHILOSOPHIC SYMBOLISM

THE composition of *Marianela* took place less than a year after the completion of the second part of *Gloria*. It also has the north coast of Spain for its setting; in fact Ficóbriga is visible from the mines of Socartes, where the action of *Marianela* transpires. Yet despite the obvious linking of the two novels in time and space, their emotional viewpoint is quite different. In *Marianela* Galdós turns away from the religious problem to tell an idyllic story of tragic love and to study the responsibilities of the rich toward the poor.

Joaquín Casalduero sensed and expressed admirably the twofold basis of the novel: "*Marianela* discurre, pues, en dos direcciones completamente distintas. De un lado tenemos el idilio entre Nela y Pablo y de otro un problema social, presentándose éste bifurcado: vida del proletariado y actitud de los ricos ante la miseria. Estos dos temas a primera vista se presentan totalmente independientes el uno del otro."[1]

Casalduero goes on to an analysis of the relationship of the idyllic element with the philosophy of Auguste Comte. He sees in the Spanish novel a reflection of the three stages in the development of mankind, stages which Comte considered fundamental to his thought: the theological, the metaphysical, and finally

[1] Joaquín Casalduero, "Auguste Comte y *Marianela*," *Smith College Studies in Modern Languages*, 21 (1939), 12.

the positivistic. Marianela, the undernourished, unlovely child-woman, who explains the world through myths invented by her imagination, represents the theological stage of the Comtian system.

After this original stage comes a transitory metaphysical period, when man tries by reason alone, without proper observation of reality, to solve the mysteries of the universe. Pablo Penáguilas, blind from birth, but possessing "un espíritu de indagación asombroso"[2] which he thinks can lead him to absolute truth, is the example of this second stage. Like Comte's metaphysical man, he makes the transition to the positivistic or scientific state when his eyes are given sight by Dr. Teodoro Golfín. Seeing brings him in contact with reality, which causes him to reverse some of his earlier judgments, most notably his former belief that his guide Nela's bodily beauty must correspond to the loveliness of her soul.

Dr. Golfín is of course the incarnation of the positivist, while Pablo's beautiful cousin Florentina reflects Comte's notion of a new religion symbolized in the Virgin Mary. This symbolism is indicated by Marianela's mistaking Florentina for the Virgin and by the numerous cases in which the author substitutes for Florentina's name expressions like "la Imaculada"[3] or "la Virgen."[4] In short, there can be no doubt that Casalduero has proved the dependence of this Galdosian novel on positivistic philosophy.

GALDOS' CONTACTS WITH POSITIVISM

It is pertinent to notice here the awakening interest in positivism in Spain beginning with the Ateneo debates of 1875–1876, summarized by Gumersindo de Azcárate in a notable speech on April 6, 1876.[5] He mentions Comte's theory of the three stages

[2] *Marianela*, p. 717 (Chap. XI). All citations from *Marianela* are from *Obras completas*, Aguilar, Vol. IV.

[3] *Marianela*, p. 728 (Chap. XV).

[4] *Ibid.*, pp. 730 and 733 (Chaps. XVI and XVII).

[5] See *Revista contemporánea*, I, 125, 246, and 523; II, 122, 253, 383, and 505; III, 125 and 350; and IV, 230 and 465. See also *Revista Europea*, VII, 239.

of human history – theological, metaphysical, and positivistic – as if they were common knowledge among his listeners.[6] The interest provoked by these debates coincides in date with statements from contemporary observers who notice about this time the beginning of a positivist "school."[7] Magazines begin to carry articles on positivism and reviews of books on the subject.[8] Comtian philosophy was then a novelty in Spain when Galdós seized upon it as the basis for *Marianela*.[9]

The new philosophy appealed to the Spanish novelist because of its renunciation of metaphysics, or in other words, its emphasis on reality with a corresponding denial of the value of imaginative speculation. Galdós thought of himself as a realist and had made even in his youthful writings, several statements to that effect.[10] These declarations can be paired with others in which Galdós speaks disdainfully of the imagination, "la loca de la casa."

While it is true that Don Benito had a powerful imagination which he could never completely dominate,[11] it is equally true that at this period of his life he was striving mightily to control it. The well-known passage in *Doña Perfecta*,[12] where Pepe Rey

[6] *Revista contemporánea*, III, 362; and IV, 475.

[7] See above, p. 47; and Menéndez Pelayo in *Revista Europea*, VIII, 466.

[8] For example, Mark Pattison, "La religión del positivismo" in *Revista Contemporánea*, III, 50; Littré, *Los progresos del positivismo*, *ibid*., VII, 99; P. Estasen, *Noción del derecho según la filosofía positiva*, *ibid*., VII, 505; R. Schiattarella, *Auguste Comte y Macleod*, *ibid*., IX, 145; and a review of A. Poey's *El positivismo*, in *Revista Europea*, VII, 117.

[9] Galdós himself was aware of positivism much earlier. In an article dated Jan. 30, 1872, he speaks of Littré's election to the French Academy and mentions Comte as the father of positivism. See W. H. Shoemaker (ed.), *Crónica de la quincena*, p. 73. Again, on May 15, 1872, he calls attention to ". . . los estragos que en entendimientos muy ilustrados hace la escuela positivista . . ." (*ibid*., p. 131), showing a lack of sympathy for the movement at this stage of his development.

[10] In his essay *El Sol* (*cf*. H. Chonin Berkowitz, *Pérez Galdós – Spanish Liberal Crusader*, p. 34); in the *Revista de España*, XV (1870), 162; in the *Crónica de la quincena* (Jan. 15, 1872) he says: "No hay cosa alguna más hermosa que la realidad . . ." (Shoemaker, *op. cit*., p. 62); and in a personal letter (written in 1871) he speaks of raising the banner of reality in protest against a depraved realism (Berkowitz, *op. cit*., p. 93).

[11] Shoemaker, *op. cit*., pp. 43-46.

[12] *Obras completas*, Aguilar, IV, 416.

exclaims: "La fantasía, la terrible loca, que era el ama de la casa, pasa a ser criada . . . Dirija usted la vista a todos lados, señor penitenciario, y verá el admirable conjunto de realidad que ha sustituído a la fábula," certainly foreshadows the theme of *Marianela*[13] and shows clearly Galdós' desire to replace imagination with observation.

Galdós was not, of course, indifferent to the literary trends of his times. To be a realist during his early years meant to be opposed to the "idealistic" novel, that is, the novel of imaginary events and characters.[14] But up to the writing of *La desheredada* (1881), Galdós did not succeed in adopting the viewpoint of a realistic observer. Instead he mixed "idealism," specifically the abstract ideas which he incorporates in his chief characters, with a composite picture of objective reality.[15]

In *Marianela* he has not abandoned this "abstract" technique even though he uses it to show that imagination (i.e., mythological explanations of phenomena) must give way to scientific realism, as symbolized by the death of Marianela when Pablo's eyes are opened to reality. It is with regret that Galdós sees the destruction of beautiful, but warped and untrue, fantasy[16] and the triumph of positivistic thought. He was attracted to positivism because it was in his opinion true, because it supported his realistic position, and because it was a popular novelty of the period, but at the same time he saw regretfully that the charm of fantasy must be sacrificed.

[13] As noticed by Casalduero, *op. cit.*, p. 21.

[14] Galdós stated this opposition of idealism and realism clearly in 1870 (*Revista de España*, XV, 162–163): ". . . los españoles somos poco observadores, y carecemos por lo tanto de la principal virtud para la creación de la novela moderna . . . somos unos idealistas desaforados, y más nos agrada imaginar que observar." *Cf.* Sherman Eoff, "The Spanish Novel of 'Ideas': Critical Opinion," PMLA, LV (1940), 531–558.

[15] Casalduero, *Vida y obra de Galdós*, Losada, Buenos Aires, 1943, pp. 50–65; see also Revilla's statement below, p. 137, n. 2.

[16] *Cf.* ". . . ah! la superstición, estado de la conciencia que embelesa y arrulla las almas con deliciosas mentiras," (*Memorias*, in *Obras completas*, Aguilar, VI, 1749). Compare this with Pablo's speech to Marianela: "Tus disparates, con serlo tan grandes, me cautivan, porque revelan el candor de tu alma y la fuerza de tu fantasía" (Marianela, 701).

PHILOSOPHY IN *MARIANELA* AND *WILHELM MEISTER*

While examining the books in Galdós' personal library I came upon a copy of Goethe's *Wilhelm Meister* (traduction complète et nouvelle par M. Théophile Gautier fils, 3 vols., Paris, Charpantier, 1861), which contains many marked passages, some of which I believe have a direct bearing on the conception of *Marianela*. Of particular importance is the chapter in which Wilhelm Meister, in the course of his visit to the Pedagogic Province, asks for and receives an explanation of the religious training given the boys of the region. Not one, but three religions are taught and practiced. The old men in charge of the boys' education show Wilhelm how the boys are led through the three religions much as humanity itself progresses in its various stages of development (paralleling the Comtian steps in human development).

The object of all three religions is to inspire reverence – the first, of things above, or God; the second, of one's fellowmen; and the third, of things below, such as the humble and poor, the wretched and suffering. The three religions are called respectively the Ethnic, the Philosophical, and the Christian. All three are practiced by the mature man; in fact, the creed which professes belief in God the Father, God the Son, and God the Holy Spirit is really a declaration of belief in the Ethnic, the Christian, and the Philosophical religions.[17]

Galdós has marked and annotated these paragraphs. He called attention to "La religion qui repose sur le respect de ce qui est au-dessus de nous, nous l'appelons *ethnique*; c'est la religion *des peuples*" by drawing a line in the margin, by underlining the words I have italicized, and by making the note "1°" in the margin.

In a similar way he marked "La religion qui a pour base le respect de nos égaux, nous l'appelons *philosophique*, car le phi-

[17] In the edition of *Wilhelm Meister* cited, pp. 300–302 (*Années de Voyage*, Book II, Chap. 2). In the Carlyle translation this chapter is the tenth of the *Wanderjahre*; however in the German original it is Book II, Chap. I.

losophe qui se place dans la religion moyenne fait descendre vers lui ce qui est audessus de lui, fait monter ce qui est audessous, et ce n'est que dans cette situation intermédiaire qu'il mérite le nom de sage." Opposite this passage he has not only put "2°" but also a much more significant note: "Parece que ésta debiera ser la 3ª por cuanto comprende las otras dos. Vemos, por otra parte, en la Historia, que al *paganismo* sigue el *cristianismo*, y a éste, el humanismo presente."

A little later, in the description of the third religion "qui s'appuie sur le respect de ce qui est audessous de nous; nous l'appelons *chrétienne* . . ." Galdós marked the words we have just cited and jotted "3°" in the margin. Finally a page further on, when the old men explain that the Creed declares the three religions, Galdós marked the paragraph and wrote in the margin: "D.P. [Dios Padre] = Jupiter; D.H. [Dios Hijo] = Cristo; D.E.S. [Dios Espíritu Santo] = Humanidad."

Although we have examined only a small fraction of the marked passages in *Wilhelm Meister*, we have seen enough to link Galdós' interpretation of Goethe's three religions and Comte's three stages of human development. Galdós underlined the statement that the first religion, the Ethnic, is the "*religion des peuples*" corresponding to the pastoral, primitive simplicity which he describes in Marianela's beliefs: "La Nela tiene imaginación . . . se halla en la situación de los pueblos primitivos—afirmó Teodoro—. Está en la época del pastoreo." [18] Later Galdós comments on this passage, saying: "Exacta era la idea de Teodoro Golfín al comparar el espíritu de la Nela con los pueblos primitivos. Como en éstos, dominaba en ella el sentimiento y la fascinación de lo maravilloso; creía en poderes sobrenaturales, distintos del único y grandioso Dios . . ." [19]

Then with regard to the second religion, which for Goethe is the Philosophic, Galdós corrects the German's system to make it correspond to that of Auguste Comte. The Philosophic religion should be the third stage, he says, since history shows us

[18] *Marianela*, p. 712 (Chap. IX).
[19] *Ibid.*, p. 721 (Chap. XIII).

that man goes through the steps of paganism, Christianity, and finally "humanismo." This classification is reinforced by Galdós' final note where he equates the three persons of the Trinity to Jupiter, Christ, and Humanity.[20]

The bonds we have examined between *Marianela* and *Wilhelm Meister* would not of themselves be completely convincing. It could easily be argued that Galdós, knowing Comtian philosophy, annotated his copy of Goethe but forgot completely about this passage when he came to compose *Marianela*, going back directly to Comte's writings for the positivism he puts into his novel. But there are other links between the German and Spanish works which greatly strengthen our case.

THE IDYLLIC ELEMENT

In Clarín's review of *Marianela* he informs us that "Marianela y Mignon se parecen, miradas con cierto cristal, como dos gotas de rocío," although, he goes on to say, a close comparison of the texts shows them to be different.[21] Manuel de la Revilla also finds that Marianela ". . . ofrece muchos puntos de semejanza con Mignon . . ."[22] Twenty years later Menéndez Pelayo said that in Marianela ". . . se ve el reflejo del episodio de Mignon . . ."[23] Three astute critics, all of whom knew Galdós and the literary atmosphere of the time, agree that *Wilhelm Meister* and *Marianela* have a point of contact in Mignon.

Galdós' personal copy of Goethe's work bears out their contention. There are many markings in passages referring to Wil-

[20] The equation of positivism with the adoration of humanity is by no means impossible. Galdós could have read the following statements about Comte in one of his books: ". . . c'est l'humanité qui est l'objet de son adoration . . . Il s'intitule le *grand prêtre de l'humanité*" (Laurant, *Histoire du droit des gens*, XVIII, 188–189). Furthermore the article of Mark Pattison, "La religión del positivismo," which appeared in Spanish in April 1876 talks of the religion of humanity and states that Humanity is the Supreme Being. See *Revista Contemporánea*, III, 53 and 74. A Galdosian character, José Bailón, also preaches that God is Humanity (*Torquemada en la hoguera, Obras completas*, Aguilar, V, 914), perhaps a remote recollection of Comte's idea.

[21] *Galdós*, Madrid, 1912, p. 64.

[22] Review of *Marianela* in *Revista Contemporánea*, XIV (1878), 508.

[23] M. Menéndez Pelayo, *Obras completas*, ed. Artigas, X, 97.

helm's foster daughter, most notably in the chapter (*Années d'apprentissage*, Book VIII, Chapter 9) which deals with Mignon's parents and the mystery of her birth. At the head of this section Galdós wrote "todo," indicating his interest in the entire chapter. Besides penciling nine passages in the chapter, he also wrote two more marginal notes, a very unusual practice with him. In other parts of the work there are four more marked passages dealing totally with Mignon, besides others in which she figures incidentally.

We can be sure that Galdós was interested in Mignon, but we must check the two heroines against each other to see what influence Mignon may have had on la Nela. In each case we have a physically underdeveloped girl-woman,[24] in appearance about twelve years old,[25] but in reality old enough to fall passionately in love. Each one is physically a combination of attractive and unattractive qualities: a well-proportioned although stunted body,[26] an appealing nose but a thin-lipped, tightly-closed mouth.[27].

Each girl gives the impression of an elfin, spritelike creature. This is accentuated in Mignon's case by her constant preference for boy's clothing and her childhood wanderings through the rough terrain around Lago Maggiore. Marianela's rags are those of primitive man rather than the beggar; [28] she, too, is seen against a background of nature, especially in her attempts to interpret the meaning of the flowers, the stars, and the voice of underground waters in the Trascava. Both girls are vivacious in expression and action, fond of dancing, leaping, climbing, and swinging from trees,[29] and especially of singing. In fact Marianela

[24] Mignon is regularly called a "child"; the doctor refers to her "half-developed" nature (*Wilhelm Meister, Apprenticeship*, Bk. 8, Chap. 3); Marianela is called a "niña con años y alma de mujer" (*Marianela*, p. 723; Chap. XIV) and "la mujer-niña" (*ibid.*, pp. 737 and 742; Chap. XIX).

[25] *W. M. Apprenticeship*, Bk. 2, Chap. 4; *Marianela*, p. 689 (Chap. III).

[26] Mignon is well formed but small; Marianela is "admirablemente proporcionada" but stunted (*ibid.*).

[27] *W. M. Apprenticeship*, Bk. 2, Chap. 4; *Marianela*, pp. 689–690 (Chap. III).

[28] *Marianela*, p. 689 (Chap. III).

[29] After Mignon's sickness she complains that she can climb and leap no more although she longs to climb hills and envies the birds their flight

is first presented to us by her song, which, though only a simple folksong of the Cantabrian region, moves and exalts Teodoro Golfín strangely. This corresponds to the profoundly moving "Connaît-tu le pays . . ." – not, to be sure, our first introduction to Mignon, but an early and extremely skillful means of fixing her character.[30]

Both heroines live on the fringe of society, a condition symbolized by their lack of education, their lack of economic security and family relations, and their lack of religious instruction. Each one supplies these deficiencies as best she can, and each is drawn, in respect to religion, into especially close relations with the Virgin Mary. To each one – and this is important – the Virgin appears in a vision.[31] Mignon swears a sacred oath to the Virgin not to reveal her past life, while Marianela hopes that the Virgin will endow her with physical beauty.

The two heroines receive little or no kindness from the world until they encounter Wilhelm and Pablo. Each one then falls in love with her benefactor. Wilhelm, thinking of Mignon as a mere child, promises that he will keep her always with him,[32] whereas Pablo promises marriage.[33] Then rivals appear and both Mignon and Marianela are plunged into jealous despair, which in turn brings on a physical decline and ultimately death. The men – Pablo and Wilhelm – are declared responsible for the tragic death of the two young women.[34] The latter are both buried in splendid tombs with impressive rituals.[35] Posthumously

(*Apprenticeship*, Bk. 8, Chap. 3). This passage was marked by Galdós. It parallels Marianela's vivacious dancing, swinging from branches, and longing to be a bird (*Marianela*, pp. 699, 700, and 702; Chaps. VI and VII).

[30] *Apprenticeship*, Bk. 3, Chap. 1; *Marianela*, p. 684 (Chap. I). Galdós marked Mignon's song in his copy of *Wilhelm Meister*. Clarín felt this same relationship and said, "¿Qué cantaba Marianela? Yo creo que, sin saber cómo, debía cantar aquello de ¿ *Kennst du das Land wo die Citronen glhunn* [*sic*]? que era la canción de la Marianela alemana, de Mignon inmortal."

[31] *Apprenticeship*, Bk. 8, Chap. 3; *Marianela*, p. 724 (Chap. XIV).

[32] *Apprenticeship*, Bk. 2, Chap. 14, end (this marked by Galdós); also Bk. 3, Chap. 11.

[33] *Marianela*, p. 708 (Chap. VIII).

[34] *Apprenticeship*, Bk. 8, Chap. 5; *Marianela*, p. 751 (Chap. XXI).

[35] *Apprenticeship*, Bk. 8, Chap. 9; *Marianela*, pp. 752–753 (Chap. XXII).

Mignon is discovered to be of a noble Italian family. This corresponds to Galdós' ironic epilogue in which he has English tourists invent high family and social connections for Marianela.

There is, then, a fundamental parallelism between Marianela and Mignon. Of course this does not mean that there are not numerous differences. In general Marianela is shown to be a typical case, for Galdós makes Dr. Golfín exclaim: "Como la Nela hay muchos miles de seres en el mundo,"[36] and he explains that her ideas on nature and religion are common among the uneducated Spanish peasantry.[37] Mignon is much more the exceptional case. She is also much more mysterious, as the author holds back an explanation of the circumstances of her birth and exile from home until after her death. The Italian girl is also more beautiful and more musically inclined than the Spanish one.

In view of the parallels between Marianela and Mignon and between the three stages of cultural growth of man shown both in *Wilhelm Meister* and in Galdós' novel, and especially in view of the interest in these phases of Goethe's novel shown by Galdós' markings in his personal copy, I think we can safely conclude that the reading of *Wilhelm Meister* was one of the chief sources of inspiration for *Marianela.*[38]

HUMANITARIANISM AND HUGO

While we have accounted for the idyllic element of Galdós' novel, there still remains unexplained the other current, the social problem of poverty and the attitude of the wealthy toward the poor, which we saw that Casalduero had correctly felt and

[36] *Marianela,* p. 747 (Chap. XXI).
[37] *Ibid.,* p. 722 (Chap. XIII).
[38] That Galdós understood his characters in terms of the progress of mankind is especially evident in a passage where Dr. Golfín says of la Nela: "Pero ella está hecha para realizar en poco tiempo grandes progresos y ponerse al nivel de nosotros. Alúmbresele un poco, y recorrerá con paso gigantesco los siglos . . . está muy atrasada, ve poco; pero teniendo luz, andará . . . Nosotros enseñaremos la verdad a esta pobre criatura, resucitado ejemplar de otros siglos; le haremos conocer las dotes del alma; la traeremos a nuestro siglo . . ." (*ibid.,* p. 748; Chap. XXI).

recorded. Notice that Don Joaquín says that the two themes—idyll and social problem—seem at first sight totally independent of each other. Here we sense a double source of inspiration, as two different emotional effects upon the reader have been said to correspond to two separate fountains of inspiration.[39]

Moreover the facts we gathered about Galdós' creative process in studying *Gloria* show that the Spanish novelist brought together, amalgamated, or at least juxtaposed suggestions from numerous sources in the course of his literary creation. Such was felt to be the case with *Marianela* by some of the contemporary critics. We have cited fragments of their opinions; now let us examine them *in toto*.

Revilla says that despite many beauties, *Marianela* is not Galdós' best work. "Su protagonista ofrece muchos puntos de semejanza con Mignon, Quasimodo, Gwymplaine o Gilliatt; los amores de la fea con el ciego recuerdan demasiado los de la ciega Dea y el Hombre que Ríe . . . La talla de esa figura es exagerada, y excede de los límites de lo real. El Sr. Galdós, al pintarla, se ha acordado más de Víctor Hugo que de sus modelos ingleses." [40]

Menéndez Pelayo's complete thought on *Marianela* is much the same as Revilla's. He says, ". . . *Marianela* . . . menos original quizá que otras cosas de Pérez Galdós, pero más poético y delicado: en el cual, por una parte, se ve el reflejo del episodio de Mignon en *Wilhelm Meister*, y por otra parte aquel procedimiento antitético familiar a Víctor Hugo, combinando en un tipo de mujer la fealdad de cuerpo y la hermosura de alma, el abandono y la inocencia." [41] Both of these critics point to Victor Hugo as the source of Galdós' sentimental humanitarianism.

It will be recalled that the later romantic novel—of the type popularized by Eugène Sue, and continued by Hugo in such works as *Les Misérables*—has a heroine whose misadventures incite tearful pity toward her and indignation toward her oppressors. She is normally a poor girl who strives to support herself

[39] See p. 107, n. 368.
[40] *Revista Contemporánea,* XIV (1878), 508.
[41] Menéndez Pelayo, *Obras completas,* ed. Artigas, X, 97.

by grueling hours of needlework. Society itself seems to conspire against her gaining an honest living. A villain, generally either a nobleman or a priest, offers her an easy living in exchange for her virtue. When she rejects him he then tries to gain by force what he failed to gain by money and persuasion. Ultimately the hero, who is by exception a *good* nobleman, rescues and marries the heroine.

We scarcely need to comment here on the great popularity of the sentimentally humanitarian novel in Spain and to point out that Galdós followed its pattern in parts of some of his early works. Furthermore, its unreality becomes an object of his satire in such later novels as *La desheredada* and especially *Tormento*.

Galdós certainly knew that one of the principal variations on the heroine of this type of novel was the girl with the stunted body but lovely soul, bringing in the romantic antithesis noted in our citation from Menéndez y Pelayo. Such is the case with the hunchback heroine of *Le Juif Errant*, a work which we have seen as a minor influence in *Gloria*[42] and to which we shall return soon in respect to *Marianela*. Dea, the heroine of *L'Homme qui rit*, opposes her blindness and helplessness (although not ugliness) to her spiritual beauty. But in my opinion, by far the most influential example of Hugo's antithesis of unlovely body versus lovely soul occurs in *Les Misérables*, where not one, but two girls offer analogies with la Nela.

Cosette, Hugo's heroine, is left by her mother in the care of the Thénardier family, who proceed to abuse, mistreat, and overwork the little girl until she becomes pale, ugly, and thin. Her place in the family is on a level with, or even below, the domestic animals. "On la nourrit des restes de tout le monde, un peu mieux que le chien, un peu plus mal que le chat."[43]

[42] See above, p. 90, n. 296.

[43] *Oeuvres complètes de Victor Hugo*, Hetzel et Quantin, Paris, n.d., Vol. 33, p. 278 (*Les Misérables*, Vol. I, Livre 4, Chap. 3). Compare "Éponine et Azelma ne regardaient pas Cosette. C'était pour elles comme le chien" (*Oeuvres complètes de Victor Hugo*, Vol. 34, p. 180; *Les Misérables*, Vol.

La Nela, too, was fed casually like an animal and ate her scraps seated on the floor. No one ever gave her a kind word, which even the cat received, so that her category in the Centeno family was definitely below the animals: "Todo le demostraba que su jeraquía dentro de la case era inferior a la del gato, cuyo lomo recibía blandas caricias, y a la del mirlo, que saltaba gozoso en su jaula."[44]

There is no space for either girl in the house in which she lives, so Cosette retreats to a sort of lair under the table[45] and sleeps under the stairs,[46] while Marianela is driven from one corner to another and finally makes a bed out of two large baskets.[47] In both cases the girls' plight is sharply contrasted with the opulence of the daughters of the family, whose mothers treat them relatively well.[48]

Both authors are scandalized because their heroines are forced to go barefooted,[49] which, in Galdós' case, would not be surprising except for the fact that the well-treated Centeno girls also have no shoes[50] and this, we judge, is true of almost all the peasants and workers in the Socartes mines. Certainly the Centeno girls' lack of shoes inspires no pity in their creator; hence we suspect that the compassion originating from la Nela's bare feet is a reflection of Hugo's emotion. Cosette, like Marianela, is also uneducated and uninstructed in religion.[51]

What I have been saying refers to the childhood years of Cosette. After Jean Valjean rescues her from the Thénardier

II, Livre 3, Chap. 8). Also, speaking of a different character, Marius, who lives in the same household with his unloving aunt, Hugo says: ". . . Marius n'était plus pour elle qu'une espèce de silhouette noire et vague; et elle avait fini par s'en occuper beaucoup moins que du chat ou du perroquet qu'il est probable qu'elle avait" (*Oeuvres complètes de Victor Hugo*, Vol. 35, p. 199; *Les Misérables*, Vol. III, Livre 5, Chap. 3).

[44] *Marianela*, p. 696 (Chap. IV, end).

[45] *Les Misérables*, ed. cited, I, 278; II, 147, 175, 178, and 190. Her habitual place under the table is called a "niche" and a "trou."

[46] *Ibid.*, II, 197.

[47] *Marianela*, p. 692 (Chap. IV).

[48] *Les Misérables*, I, 279; *Marianela*, p. 695 (Chap. IV).

[49] *Les Misérables*, II, 181; *Marianela*, pp. 711–712 (Chap. IX).

[50] *Marianela*, p. 695 (Chap. IV).

[51] *Les Misérables*, II, 170 and 176; *Marianela*, pp. 721–722 (Chap. XIII).

family, she grows into an entirely different person, becoming a remarkably beautiful young woman. But another character of *Les Misérables* takes over the role she formerly played. Éponine Thénardier has become a ragged and ugly waif: "C'était une créature hâve, chétive, décharnée; rien qu'une chemise et une jupe sur une nudité frissonante et glacée. Pour ceinture une ficelle, pour coiffure une ficelle, des épaules pointues sortant de la chemise, une pâleur blonde et lymphatique, des mains rouges, la bouche entr'ouverte et dégradée, des dents de moins, l'oeil terne, hardi et bas, les formes d'une jeune fille avortée et le regard d'une vielle femme corrompue . . ." [52]

This young woman, who as a well-dressed and spoiled child had spurned and mistreated Cosette, now develops at least one good character trait. She unselfishly watches over and aids Marius in his love affair with Cosette,[53] although to do this she has to sacrifice her own hopeless love for the hero. She cannot help suffering from his happiness.[54] Finally she dies, and although the circumstances are quite different from those of Marianela's death, the emotion evoked by her unhappy love and her sacrifice of herself for her rival is identical to that of Marianela's death scene.[55]

It is evident that if Éponine becomes equated to la Nela, the now radiantly beautiful Cosette plays the role of Florentina. However, the resemblance is only a general one. I think we shall find a character in *Le Juif Errant* who shows analogies to Florentina in a considerable number of details.

There is, however, another specific resemblance between the two novels we have been studying. In each one appears a family which the author uses as a vehicle to criticize the worst traits of the common people. Note that both authors are without question favorably disposed toward the poor and humble classes and do not hesitate to state their position in the works we are considering.[56] They both look on society as responsible in a large degree

[52] *Les Misérables*, III, 291.
[53] *Ibid.*, IV, 91–93.
[54] *Ibid.*, IV, 94.
[55] *Ibid.*, IV, 563–564.
[56] *Ibid.*, III, 38; *Marianela*, pp. 714–715 (Chap. X).

for the degradation of the poor, and both feel that education of the common people would soon result in the elevation of the class.[57] In view of these opinions, it is particularly significant that they have made the Thénardier and Centeno families despicable and have not sought to explain their baseness and avarice by shifting the blame onto society.

In details there are many similarities between the two groups. Both families were originally wandering peddlers, the Centenos making a miserable living by selling pots,[58] while the Thénardiers followed the army with a canteen,[59] selling, begging, and even stealing. After each family settles down, its prime interest is money, although the hard luck of the Thénardiers keeps them from amassing wealth. Mme Thénardier loves her two daughters but not her sons.[60]

Here we have a most interesting comparison to Galdós' work. The Centeno daughters are well treated; the elder son, although almost an idiot, is reasonably well treated; but the younger son, Celipín, is for no good reason made to sleep curled up on the kitchen floor upon some ragged blankets.[61] Now the hatred of Mme Thénardier falls particularly upon one of her sons, Gavroche, who leaves home to become a *gamain*,[62] just as Celipín leaves home to lead a picaresque existence in Madrid. Although his later experiences have no similarity to Hugo's character, Celipín, as he is initially presented, seems to have been suggested to Galdós by Gavroche. Only in this way can we explain why his mother treats him so differently from her other children.

A final suggestion from the Thénardier family may perhaps be found in the subordination of one spouse to the other. In the French novel it is the husband who is astute and sly and who dominates absolutely his stolid, brutish wife;[63] in the Spanish

[57] *Les Misérables*, I, 28 and 493–494; III, 29; *Marianela*, pp. 712–713 and 741 (Chaps. IX and XIX).

[58] *Marianela*, p. 694 (Chap. IV).

[59] *Les Misérables*, II, 139.

[60] *Ibid.*, I, 279; II, 142.

[61] *Marianela*, p. 693 (Chap. IV).

[62] *Les Misérables*, III, 29ff, and IV, 539ff.

[63] *Ibid.*, II, 142.

novel the roles are reversed, the wife possessing a low cleverness while the husband is about on a plane with the mules which are in his charge.[64]

In summary, we can say that the humanitarian theme of *Marianela* very likely owes much to *Les Misérables.* Not only does Hugo state his belief in, and sympathy for, the common people in abstract terms, but he also embodies them in his characters. The ugly Cosette, abused by the Thénardier family, evokes our pity just as does the stunted Marianela, unloved and unwanted by the Centenos. Later, Éponine's self-sacrifice recalls Nela's abnegation. The Thénardier and Centeno families show a similar conception. And the two boys, Gavroche and Celipín, who react to maternal harshness by becoming *pícaros,* are particularly worthy of note.

The influence of Hugo is, however, by no means limited to that provided by *Les Misérables.* Revilla called special attention to *L'Homme qui rit,* which is a humanitarian novel utilizing the old elements in different combinations. Gwymplaine, the hero, has been disfigured in boyhood to make him into a clown. His mouth was slit to the ears, causing his face to be distorted into a perpetual laugh, but giving him a hideous expression which produced horror in most women. Dea, the heroine, was blind and for her Gwymplaine was beautiful,[65] as she saw only his soul.[66] The very fact that he repeatedly says he is ugly[67] makes her state that seeing prevents one from arriving at the truth.

> —Voir? qu'appelez-vous voir, vous autres? Moi je ne vois pas, je sais. Il paraît que voir, cela cache.
> —Que veux-tu dire? demanda Gwymplaine.
> Dea répondit: —Voir est une chose qui cache le vrai.
> —Non, dit Gwymplaine.
> —Mais si! répliqua Dea, puisque tu dis que tu es laid![68]

[64] *Marianela,* p. 695 (Chap. IV).
[65] *Oeuvres complètes de Victor Hugo,* Hetzel et Quantin, Paris, 1883, Vol. 40, pp. 411 and 458.
[66] *Ibid.,* p. 414.
[67] For example, *ibid.,* p. 432.
[68] *Ibid.,* p. 434.

In similar words Pablo declares that Marianela must be beautiful. "Lo digo yo, que poseo una verdad inmutable . . . El don de la vista puede causar grandes extravíos . . . aparta a los hombres de la posesión de la verdad absoluta . . . y la verdad absoluta dice que tu eres hermosa . . ." [69]

The idyllic love of the ugly man with the beautiful soul and the lovely but blind girl ends with the death of the girl, killed by the sorrow brought on by her lover's supposed death and the joy occasioned by his return. Another character accuses Gwymplaine of having killed her,[70] just as Teodoro Golfín accuses Pablo of having killed la Nela and as Wilhelm Meister blames himself for Mignon's death.

DETAILS FROM *THE WANDERING JEW*

Agricol, the hero of Eugène Sue's work, is a handsome, poetically inclined laborer. He has been brought up in childhood companionship with la Mayeux, an almost hunchbacked girl with a pale and pock-marked face. She, like Marianela, possesses a sweet and lofty spirit, and in addition she has a far more cultivated mind than the Spanish heroine. As the children grow up Agricol continues to regard her as an adopted sister, although la Mayeux develops a secret and almost hopeless love for him.[71] About this time Agricol meets a young noblewoman of dazzling beauty, in whom la Mayeux sees a rival. The noblewoman, Adrienne, is in some ways the counterpart of Florentina in Galdós' novel. After she meets la Mayeux she soon comes to esteem the loveliness of her soul and ultimately undertakes to care for her. She wants la Mayeux always to live with her, just as Florentina wants to make a sister of la Nela.[72] The plan does not work out in Adrienne's case, owing to her premature death.

In this situation, which could well have been inspired in Galdós by Eugène Sue, there is a detail which the former seems to have

[69] *Marianela*, p. 704 (Chap. VII).
[70] *Ibid.*, Vol. 41, p. 461.
[71] *Le Juif Errant*, Part V, Chap. 5.
[72] *Ibid.*, Part XVI, Chap. 21.

transferred from one character to another, just as the blindness of Hugo's heroine Dea is transferred to Galdós' hero Pablo. Adrienne loves beauty passionately;[73] in Galdós' work this trait is given to Marianela. Adrienne finds la Mayeux physically repulsive at first; Marianela, because of her belief that only beautiful things have a right to existence and happiness, feels that she and Florentina can never be friends. Thus the importance which is given to beauty separates temporarily the women in both of the novels.

These generalities can, of course, be similarities brought on merely by the fact that the two novels belong to the same general type. But there is one other detail which involves a closer parallelism. Both Sue and Galdós portray a well-to-do woman who lavishes her affection on her dog and who places the dog's comfort and safety above that of poor human beings. When Mme Grivois' dog bites a dyer on his dye-stained wrist the lady's concern is all for the dog, whom she fears may be poisoned by the dye.[74] Galdós portrays a scene in which Marianela, with thoughts of suicide in her mind, goes down a slippery slope to the edge of an abyss. Doña Sofía's pet dog runs after her and the lady's only fear is that the dog may fall into the pit. The only reason why she scolds la Nela for going down to a dangerous place is because the dog would surely follow and be in peril.[75] The emotional tone and satirical purpose of the two passages are identical.

It is not necessarily proven that Galdós found inspiration either consciously or unconsciously in *Le Juif Errant*, but in any case, he did use situations and characters which abound in all novels of the sentimentally humanitarian type. Because Galdós surely knew this immensely popular novel, I incline to believe that he patterned the relationship of Florentina to Marianela and the inhuman dog-loving woman after its counterparts. But it is obvious that he did not copy slavishly; his chief borrowing is the over-all emotional effect of the two situations.

[73] *Ibid.*, Part II, Chap. 4.
[74] *Ibid.*, Part VIII, Chap. 4.
[75] *Marianela*, pp. 710–711 (Chap. IX).

The foregoing pages give the impression that *Marianela* resulted from the relatively simple combination of three elements—*Wilhelm Meister*, positivism, and the humanitarian novel. It is now my intention to show that the process was more complicated than it appears at first sight and to suggest what may have been the order in which the various elements entered the combination.

Because Galdós made a declaration of faith in human progress through science and industrialism in the character of Pepe Rey (dating from the spring of 1876) we can assume that he was attracted to positivism by that time. We must associate Pepe Rey's statements of positivism with the new interest in Comte, provoked especially by the Ateneo debates during the preceding winter. Among other things, positivism taught Galdós a new concept of realism, a much greater reliance on observation and a great diminution of the importance of the speculative faculties (fantasy and imagination). He himself could say with Pablo Penáguilas: "También la imaginación habla . . . La mía a veces se pone tan parlanchina que tengo que mandarla callar,"[76] or with León Roch, "¡Desgraciados los que no logran encadenar su imaginación!"[77] Galdós' disdain of the imagination is the reverse of his admiration for scientific truth and literary realism.

The plot of *Marianela* is not intimately bound to its setting. The events of the story could have taken place almost anywhere. But there does seem to be one good reason on the philosophical level for the selection of the mining region: Galdós wishes to contrast industrialism with the patriarchal simplicity of agriculture. If the latter has its charm, the former has its epic qualities, heretofore completely overlooked by the Spaniards. Despite the fact that the miners seek so prosaic a thing as silicate of zinc, from which pots and pans are made, this mineral nevertheless contributes greatly to well-being and civilization. "¡Oh! La hojalata tiene también su epopeya."[78] And the little village of Aldeacorba

[76] *Marianela*, p. 707 (Chap. VIII).
[77] *Obras completas*, Aguilar, IV, 776 (Pt. I, Chap. VII).
[78] *Marianela*, p. 697 (Chap. V).

de Suso, most of whose houses have been destroyed so that the mines may be enlarged, represents the old giving way to the new. Pablo says, "Nuestros padres vivían sobre miles de millones sin saberlo";[79] and although the old life was pleasant, it must give way to the less charming advantages derived from science and industrialism, just as imagination must yield to realism.[80] The theme of industrialism is a facet of positivism.

Not long before the writing of *Marianela*, Galdós must have visited the mines of Reocín. They are about three miles west of Torrelavega, which is Galdós' Villamojada, the railway station and market town for both Socartes and Ficóbriga (i.e. Santillana del Mar). Reocín lies about three quarters of a mile above the old town of Cartes in mountains known as la Sierra de Cartes. Hence the name Socartes. A mile and a quarter up the river Besaya from Cartes is Riocorbo, which must have suggested the name Aldeacorba. I have personally checked the topographical details of Socartes against Reocín and I believe the former is rather closely modeled on the latter,[81] although Galdós stressed and heightened the picturesque elements and perhaps recombined them for a more impressive effect, just as he did with the real topography which he combined into Ficóbriga.

Philosophy and topography could never have produced a novel all by themselves. Something was needed to bring them and other elements together and to give the spark to kindle the whole. This something was undoubtedly *Wilhelm Meister*. As Galdós read of the three religions in the Pedagogic Province, he thought of Comte, "le grand prêtre de l'humanité," and annotated the passage to give the religion of humanity precedence over Christianity. He also began to glimpse a wild sprite, somewhat like

[79] *Ibid.*, p. 688 (Chap. II).

[80] It is possible that Galdós observed some young woman at the mines of Reocín who incited his pity and became associated in his mind with Mignon and the heroines of the humanitarian novels. Even more likely is the supposition that the brutalizing life of the miner in general suggested the mines as a setting for a humanitarian story.

[81] See *Enciclopedia Universal*, Calpe, L, 889–890; LXII, 1328 (with picture of the Reocín mines); Rodrigo Amador de los Ríos, *Santander*, Barcelona, 1891, pp. 841 and 843; and Julián Fresnedo de la Calzada, *Santander y su provincia*, Santander, 1920, pp. 24–25, 51, and 141.

Mignon, who would represent humanity in its primitive theological stage. Some of her attributes – reliance on the imagination, mythological explanations of the phenomena of the world, her uselessness in the modern world – sprang to his mind from Comtian philosophy.

But the story of Mignon produced another emotional reaction in Galdós. Our modern reactions are apt to be pity, sympathy, and an intense curiosity to know the secret of this strange creature. But while our pity and sympathy are for the individual, Galdós' were much more on a social basis. They took particularly the form of indignation against the priests and monks who blocked the marriage of Mignon's parents. Next to the paragraph telling of these events Galdós has inserted the marginal note "¡siempre miserables!";[82] a little later he wrote next to the account of a false miracle, "¡divino! contra los farsantes!";[83] in the next chapter, beside the narrative of the Protestant parson's assistance in curing the harper, Galdós noted, "contraste del pastor y el clerizonte,"[84] showing that the priest of the previous chapter was still arousing his indignation.

This is an attitude of sentimental humanitarianism, as Galdós' indignation is against those who prevented the marriage of Mignon's parents and thus made the child homeless, profoundly shaken psychologically, and finally an object of pity and sympathy. We cannot but be surprised at Galdós' reaction, so different from our own and apparently so unjust, as Mignon's parents were brother and sister and her father was already a monk.

For the moment the important point is that Galdós saw Mignon as a victim of social oppression. The priests are the villains in *Wilhelm Meister*, as were the Jesuits in *Le Juif Errant*. Here is the associative link that could join Mignon-Marianela with la Mayeux and bring her rival Florentina into being after the pattern of Adrienne. Marianela was already associated with Comte's primitive man; Adrienne-Florentina, all sympathy and generosity

[82] *Wilhelm Meister* (Traduction complète et nouvelle par M. Théophile Gautier fils), Paris, Charpantier, 1861, II, 101 (*Apprenticeship*, Bk. 8, Chap. 9).
[83] *Ibid*., p. 104.
[84] *Ibid*., p. 113.

toward the physically imperfect and impoverished rival, is immediately associated with Comte's Virgin Mary. Hence the false miracle by which la Nela sees Florentina as the Virgin, in which Galdós, although he was deliberately avoiding religious controversy because of much adverse opinion aroused by *Gloria,* cannot refrain from repeating Goethe's device "contra los farsantes." He was possibly commenting on the recent miracle of Lourdes, as Casalduero suggests,[85] in much the same way that he has Pepe Rey say: "Todos los milagros posibles se reducen a los que yo hago en mi gabinete, cuando se me antoja, con una pila de Bunsen, un hilo inductor y una aguja imantada."[86]

But when Galdós saw in Mignon a victim of social oppression his mind would instantly jump to the usual villains in such situations. The aristocrats and the wealthy are constantly cast in this role. Even society as a whole plays the unattractive part. By this association of ideas Galdós would come to Victor Hugo, whose faith in progress and the common people, belief in the power of education to transform the world, and blame of society for the faults and even crimes of the people all harmonized with the tone Galdós intended to strike in his new novel.

Having associated Marianela, and probably by this time Florentina, with two stages of man's development in the Comtian system, Galdós was now looking for characters to represent the metaphysical and positivistic levels of man. The first of these, in which man seeks to explain the universe by intelligence alone without close observation of reality, he symbolized by a blind hero. Usually Galdós' blind characters are out of touch with reality. Two notable examples are Rafael del Aguila in the Torquemada series and the Count of Albrit in *El Abuelo,* the former completely blind, the latter nearly so. This rather obvious symbolism seems to indicate that Galdós was now working from the Comtian abstraction – metaphysical man – to the character – Pablo Penáguilas. To put it another way, by the time he created

[85] "Auguste Comte y *Marianela,*" *Smith College Studies in Modern Languages,* XXI, 20.
[86] *Obras completas,* Aguilar, IV, 417 (Chap. VI).

Pablo he had already decided to mirror the Comtian system in all his principal characters.

If Galdós had recently read *Les Misérables* he would have remembered the phrase ". . . être aveugle et être aimé, c'est en effet, sur cette terre où rien n'est complet, une des formes les plus étrangement exquises du bonheur."[87] In any case he would certainly have recalled the love of the blind Dea and the ugly Gwymplaine. From this point on, Comtian philosophy imposed the main outlines of the plot upon him. Since the metaphysical state of man is transitory, passing into the positivist, Pablo must gain contact with reality by regaining his sight. Since the modern world has no use for mythology and uncontrolled speculation, Marianela must die. Pablo must choose the future beatitude represented by Florentina.

For Pablo to regain his sight (without a miracle) a doctor is necessary, and what is more natural than to make this doctor the embodiment of positivism? The doctor is almost the only man of science known to nineteenth-century Spaniards and he is almost universally a freethinker.[88]

All these elements – and with them we have everything necessary for the novel – are linked together by bonds of association. The whole process I have taken some time to describe could have happened with the rapidity of a chain reaction, in a moment of inspiration or crystallization exactly like the one in which *Gloria* was born. It seems probable that such was the case, as Galdós did not have to do much, if any, preparatory reading for this novel.

[87] *Les Misérables*, ed. cited, I, 299.

[88] Tolosa Latour, a doctor and an intimate friend of Galdós, comments on the novelist's interest in medicine as follows: "Tiene afecto hacia la medicina y los médicos. Lo prueba su buen gusto de no ridiculizarlos jamás. *Celipín* el de *Marianela* será con el tiempo el *Doctor Centeno*, y veremos cómo estudia, antes de conseguir la borla, *veterinaria* y *farmacia*; *Augusto Miquis*, el distinguido médico de *La desheredada*, es un retrato en cuerpo y alma; las escenas del *crup* en *León Roch* y la operación de *Teodoro Golfín*, el oculista, están estudiadas con exquisito cuidado y descritas de un modo sorprendente; y por fin, entre sus lectores cuenta a no pocos médicos" (*La Epoca*, March 26, 1883). It is especially interesting to see that a contemporary doctor approved of the description of the operation on Pablo's eyes, which Casalduero finds imperfect from the point of view of naturalistic technique.

CONCLUSION

We would do well to consider here the general tendencies noticed in Galdós' creation of *Gloria* and *Marianela.* Outstanding among these are the following: the deliberate search for material on the topic of the novel before its composition, the amalgamation of material from many sources by associative linking, the sorting and choosing of material because of its contribution to the over-all emotional tone the author wishes to achieve and maintain, and the predominance of now one, now another model for the same fictitious place or character.

At the time Galdós wrote *Gloria* and *Marianela,* he thought of himself as a realist as always. In fact he makes his heroine defend the realism of the picaresque novels in *Gloria.*[1] Yet his notion of realism at this time did not include the idea of a slavish copying from reality. He felt that elements from reality could and should be rearranged to enhance the interest, picturesqueness, and beauty of the thing described. This we saw clearly in the composite construction of Ficóbriga, where the main plan came from Castro Urdiales while the church was brought in from Santillana, the pine grove from Santander, and so on. And in each case the effect was more beautiful or picturesque. Galdós was still partly influenced by the so-called idealistic novel whose slogan was "Art intensifies nature." [2]

[1] *Gloria,* p. 507 (I, 6).

[2] M. de la Revilla, "Bocetos literarios – D. Benito Pérez Galdós," in *Revista Contemporánea,* XIV (1878), 123, affirms that Galdós' novels are

The same procedure is applied to most of the characters: they are composites. But as compared to earlier characters, such as those of *Doña Perfecta*, they represent a long step toward realism. No longer are they so obviously incarnated moral forces. In *Gloria*, for example, neo-Catholicism is represented not in one abstraction but in a number of living varieties. The characters of *Marianela*, even though they embody the philosophical system of Comte, disguise their origin more successfully than those of the earlier work.

An interesting comparison can be made between Galdós and Norman Douglas who, in the introduction to *South Wind*,[3] gives some account of the materials he put together in this novel. The island setting, which some correspondents had supposed to be a realistic picture of Capri, is, in his words, "two-thirds imaginary. And the remaining third of it is distilled out of several Mediterranean islands; it is a composite place." Parts of it are taken from Capri, parts from Ischia, Ponza, and the Lipari Islands. The same mixture of imagination and composite memories of many persons holds true of the characters. For example, Miss Wilberforce was put together out of some twelve real-life persons, in spite of the fact that some of Douglas' correspondents had identified her and all the other characters of the story with people then living on Capri.

I hope the reader does not feel that I have destroyed or explained away the genius of Galdós. I hope he does not now look on Galdós as a "derivative" author of secondary importance. The more light we shed on the creative process, the less mysterious it seems and the more the author is removed from the exalted, superhuman plane and brought nearer to the normal human stature. For this reason, authors instinctively tend either to hide what they know about their creative process or to emphasize the role of the imagination, the mystery factor. In this way they place the

models of perfect realism, but not that realism which is at odds with all beauty and all ideals. His realism is capable of idealizing wisely and delicately that which reality offers us.

[3] Modern Library Edition, New York, 1925.

artist – that is, themselves – in a special category of humanity and give even more distinction to their calling. Yet if we were fortunate enough to have the necessary documents, I believe we could prove that almost every work of literature is made up, as far as raw material is concerned, in exactly the way that Galdós proceeded. This would be particularly true of the use of literary "borrowings."

Théophile Gautier, to cite one case, drew heavily on various sources, including printed material. But does this make him less original? As Louise Dillingham expressed it, "He draws ideas, phrases, from various sources, and then, without regard to their provenance as such, puts them together, one after the other or intermingled one with the other, in such a manner that the whole . . . shall yet have an individual value and impress his public by its own interest, exclusive of any documentary importance which the critic may later find in it. It is, quite naturally, later critics who have called attention to the manner in which Gautier built up this whole, who have distinguished the various sources which he puts together to make his impression; to some of them his method seems deplorable, through its check to originality, to others it appears a means of true creation, in that it actually changes and makes anew the materials with which it works." [4]

In the case of Coleridge's *Rime of the Ancient Mariner*, J. L. Lowes showed that a vast amount of reading of "sources" preceded the composition and that the poem is studded with "derivative" or "borrowed" phrases. Yet Coleridge referred to it as "a work of pure imagination" and Lowes maintains that his study confirms this declaration. An artist must work with *something*, not create out of *nothing*.[5] There is really little difference between deriving material directly from reality and getting it from printed works provided that the material is used as such and is rewrought by the craftsman. The smith who forges an old piece

[4] Louise B. Dillingham, *The Creative Imagination of T. Gautier*, Princeton, N.J., Psychological Review Co., 1927, pp. 235–236.
[5] See J. L. Lowes, *The Road to Xanadu*, Boston, Houghton Mifflin, 1927, pp. 240–241.

of metal into new form, even though it retains some traces of its former state, is not less of an artist than the one who starts his artefact from a simple ingot.

Genius lies, first of all, in the delicate sensibility which forms the over-all tone of the novel and chooses, out of the masses of material available, that which conveys this feeling to the reader. In the second place, genius guides the choice of words, rhythms, and style. Thus to me genius is above all an emotional quality, and emotion has been said to be the very essence of art.

Index

INDEX